BRANDING BEYOND LOGOS

BRANDING BEYOND LOGOS: Stand Out, Sell More & Turn
Customers Into Advocates With These 17 Brand Building
Elements
Ainsley Moir

Published in Canada by Ainsley Ideas Inc.
ISBN 978-1-7753817-0-9

Great brands don't just happen.
They're engineered.
                    - Ainsley Moir

Dedication

Dedicated to everyone who ever believed in me. Your encouragement lights my soul on fire.

PREFACE

What does your *brand* say about your business?

The word "branding" gets thrown around a lot. While it's great that people know what the word is and sense that it's important to building a business, it's still loaded with ambiguity for many. The term itself, as well as a slew of other business jargon, comes across as especially vague for business owners and entrepreneurs who either don't have formal training (in the areas of branding or marketing) or minimal amounts of it—and rightly so.

Consider the woodworker who specializes in crafting beautifully-designed, locally-sourced home furnishings; the kinds of pieces which lend an air of elegance to family meals, as people sit down together around reclaimed hardwood dinner tables for the holidays. How can he or she be expected to possess expertise in that chosen trade *and* be a master at building the business through ongoing branding efforts? The same holds true for the independent scientist who spends months or years researching and developing a unique skincare product that's actually proven to reverse the signs of aging. Beakers and branding seem like an odd combination, don't they?

Odds are you're a specialist, too. Perhaps you're a writer whose artistry reveals itself in compelling stories about community leaders who've overcome adversity to get where they are today. Maybe you're a chef and restaurant owner who frequently hears that yours is "the best pasta sauce" in the entire city. Whether or not that's you—or you're the person behind the newest app everyone's raving about—I can't imagine you launched your business in hopes of dedicating a good chunk of your working hours to tasks which involve marketing and branding. It's unrealistic.

When we're good at something, as you no doubt are, it makes sense to turn that passion and talent into a revenue-generating stream of income you can call your own. Yet, without some level of business and branding know-how, all of the amazing products or services you offer wind up taking up space in your basement (as unsold merchandise) or your mind (as untapped solutions). Your expertise goes largely unnoticed, never touching the outside world the way you intended.

I've seen what true branding can do for a businesses, having spent more than a decade building some the world's most recognizable brands: Coca-Cola®, Campbell Soup Company®, V8 Juice® and Dove Soap® to name a few. These brands, while they'll never be perfect, extend beyond the names and logos which appear at eye level on your nearby supermarket shelf in the form of product packaging. What they have in common is their ability to create followers, fans, connections and advocates—by being ruthless in their efforts to protect and build, you guessed it, their brands!

The companies behind these brands excel in the areas of product development, quality control, innovation and process management. While that accounts for a part of their success, they also understand the importance of branding and staying true to their brands across everything they do. Working with these brands, I quickly learned that a commitment to brand protection is the common thread which separates great brands from all the rest.

Once I made the decision to leave being an employee behind and instead start a business to help multiple small to large companies like yours truly grow, by using the power of branding, I quickly realized three things. First, a lot of businesses think of branding as having only to do with their logos. Second, the majority of small to mid-sized and even large companies are not integrating their brands into everything they do. Third, the word *branding* means different things to different people. Even clients who understand the term have difficulty focusing on the task of staying true to their brand across everything they do, which is why they hire me.

So, stop a minute and ask what branding means to you. For many people, branding means "design work." Think logos, colors or a flyer which advertise a special offer during the holiday season. For others, the term is interchangeable with "advertising" and all the various ways there are to push your product in the market. These days it's difficult to keep from making a quick mental leap to "social media," as well, since that's where we believe most of today's advertising takes place. For others still, branding is just another bit of business jargon which doesn't carry a lot of weight: "It doesn't have anything to do with driving sales to my doorstep." Or, does it?

My goal with this book is to help you understand what a brand truly is. More importantly, I want to help you build a strong brand; one that does, in fact, drive sales and bring customers knocking at your real or virtual door. Your logo plays a role in that, sure, but your brand encompasses so much more! For you to have a brand that lasts, all of your brand-building elements need to be firing simultaneously. All of the elements you need to achieve that are laid out in this book. For you to have a vested interest in the branding effort, your approach should be as unique as your business is. Otherwise, you won't have the necessary energy or interest to follow through with upkeep.

I want you to be excited about every aspect of branding your business, so the pieces fall together in a way which energizes you and earns you a hefty return on your effort. Your existing brand, whatever stage it's at, is one thing. But no business ever remains entirely the same. Every single product or service offering changes over time. Your brand and the way you promote it today isn't necessarily a template for what it'll be in the future—and that's a good thing. As human beings, we grow and evolve. Our businesses should do the same.

If you approach this book as intended (with the knowledge that it's a tool for building your brand), you'll ultimately build a business that can't be replicated. Products and services can be replicated. The guy down the street could very well build a business that's eerily similar to yours with the intent to hone in on your market share. However, brands are not easily replicated at all. Brands are enduring: They live in the minds of consumers, employees, the public and anyone who either loves or hates what they represent. Yep, brands have that much power!

Your own brand may seem intangible now, but it's the most important asset your business has. I encourage you to think of your brand as just that: an asset. Like a piece of machinery in a factory, you'll need to tweak your brand from time to time to ensure that it's working at optimum capacity. This will also keep you from wasting your time and money (and other people's). When it's built correctly from the beginning—either engineered or re-engineered to be effective and efficient—a brand is of lasting value to you and your customers with few to no overhauls required for quite some time.

If you're in the process of starting a business, this book is a great guide for doing that correctly. If you didn't take a holistic approach to branding your business early on, this book will help you map out a plan for overhauling your current brand. The end result will be a brand that accurately portrays who you are, what your business stands for and how both can benefit new and existing customers. In short, it will help you grow your business. Even if growing your business isn't your number one concern today, it will be someday. Again, nothing in this world remains static. Letting your brand do the heavy lifting for you, during times of change, will always be of benefit to you.

What does your *brand* say about your business—today? What is a brand, anyhow? Before you read on, let's define what a brand really is. There's too much ambiguity around it already. The Web Finance, Inc., business dictionary defines a brand this way: "A unique design, sign, symbol, words or a combination of these employed in creating an image that identifies a product and differentiates it from its competitors." With time, Web Finance adds, "images take on connotations closely associated with quality, credibility and satisfaction." In that way, it helps consumers (who are forever busy and in search of shortcuts for understanding) "make sense of the benefits and value your business offers them, in an otherwise crowded and complex marketplace."

Okay, that helps. Still, it's too lengthy for my liking. What follows is my own working definition of a brand. As you read it, consider how it relates to your specific business: "The unique, ownable and identifiable representation of your product or service which touches every part of your business and encompasses everything you do—but lives primarily in people's minds and hearts."

Based on that definition, is your brand benefiting you? Do you even have one? By the end of this book, you will have engineered (or retooled) an enduring brand, which benefits you, your business and the people who will buy your brand. Each chapter of this book walks you through a specific and important aspect of the branding process, in everyday language and in ways which will help you view your product or service in new and exciting ways. After all, big business has nothing on you. Sure, I've promoted and marketed Fortune 500 brands, but start-ups and small to mid-sized businesses across countless industries need to connect with customers, too, and these businesses are the businesses of the future.

At Engineer Your Brand, my team and I help business owners like you turn prospects into loyal consumers—the kind responsible for growing your business beyond anything you previously imagined. Every day we interact with businesses offering great products and services. They're owned by woodworkers, coaches, skincare specialists, software developers, food manufacturers and others who strive to create meaningful connections with their unique clients or clients-to-be. Brand building is applicable to every form of business across every industry.

I want to help you engineer your brand in a way that frees you up to do more of what you love and more of what got you started in business. I want to help you inspire other business owners, through your example. In addition, I want you to be better equipped to weather the ups and downs that come with seeing a business through all stages and phases of its life cycle. Use this book as a guide, whether you're just launching your business or are finally ready to build a brand that clearly communicates what it is you believe in and stand for.

No matter where your business is at today or what industry you're in, this book will help you build a brand that results in meaningful connections with people who are eager to know all about you. It will help you grow a niche for yourself and stand out. It will also help by allowing you to keep doing the work you love without worrying whether there are enough customers to go around. Because, at the end of the day, none of that happens magically. Similarly, great brands don't just "happen". They're engineered to succeed.

Acknowledgements

I am who I am today because those closest to me have given me space to grow. Those who believe in me support me and encourage me—on whichever path I choose, including the writing of this book—have surrounded me throughout my life. As a result, I've been able to forge a path I'm passionate about.

Mom and Dad, your constant love and support are the greatest gifts I've ever received. Mom, thank you for teaching me to work hard for the things I want in life. I wouldn't be where I am today without that. Dad, your entrepreneurial spirit is something I'm so grateful to have passed onto me. Thank you for embracing that.

Cahill, thank you for your partnership, encouragement and support across everything I do. You remind me that I can do anything and have no reason to be afraid.

To everyone who is part of the Engineer Your Brand extended family, thank you for your dedication to greatness. You have made this book possible, by consistently showing up as your best selves. To my editor, Christine at Write Revise Edit, thank you for helping this book become real and for helping this marketer become an author.

To everyone who has ever believed in me and encouraged me, thank you. Thank you for the opportunities you've given me. Thank you for helping me find ways to make things possible. Thank you for keeping me motivated and inspired to constantly dream big.

Your Brand Is Your Purpose

What do you want your *brand* to be?

This is one of the most important questions to ask yourself, when you think about the purpose behind your brand. Others include: What do you want your brand to stand for? How should your brand make new and existing customers feel? What impact do you want your brand to have on your community, your industry and the world?

Your brand purpose ultimately translates into your mission statement or, as I prefer to think of it, your Massive Transformative Purpose or MTP for short. Feel free to think of it as your mission statement, your purpose statement or your MTP. They are all closely connected, with the primary idea behind all of them being to create a courageous goal, which clears a path to where you want to take your business. One which then helps you get there with clarity and, subsequently, greater ease. When building your brand, establishing the purpose or the reason behind your company's existence is a critical first step. It's one that'll have a monumental impact on everything you do moving forward.

Your brand is your purpose, so take time to dream BIG and be bold!

Your Massive Transformative Purpose

Let's start by laying out the basics. Of all three statement types—mission, purpose and Massive Transformative Purpose aka MTP—I've found the MTP to be the most forward-looking and the most perfectly-suited to helping my clients get where it is they want to be. I'm confident it'll do the same for you. The term was coined at Singularity University. Singularity is a think tank based in California's Silicon Valley which seeks to empower "individuals and organizations with the mindset, skillset and network to build breakthrough solutions that leverage emerging technologies" (i.e., artificial intelligence, robotics, digital biology) to solve humanity's greatest challenges.

More succinctly? Singularity is focused on carrying out what it calls "an ambitious mission to create a positive impact on our world." It leverages an abundance mindset to do that and defines MTPs as statements that are simultaneously:

- Audaciously big and aspirational (aka massive)
- Impactful to industries and individuals worldwide (aka transformative)
- Clear in their reason for being, which unites and inspires others to act (aka purposeful)

Singularity University Co-Founder Peter Diamandis heads up a number of transformational businesses and is the author of several acclaimed books. I recommend *Abundance: The Future Is Better than You Think* and *BOLD: How to Go Big, Create Wealth and Impact the World*. Diamandis sums up the essence of the MTP by saying that it comes alive when you commit to "find something you would die for—and live for it." This is such a powerful statement, and can be applied no matter what business you're in. Whether you've created a technology that revolutionizes the way humans interact with one another, launched a landscaping business that beautifies your surrounding neighborhood or created a nonprofit that aims to end world hunger, think about what you stand strongly behind. Then? Build your business and brand on that.

Ultimately, your MTP becomes your brand. That's because it lays out (with precision) what you and your business stand for or what motivates you to do what you're doing. In order to be its most effective, your brand should revolve around that. If you stand for service, your MTP might speak to providing high levels of customer care. How your brand approaches and connects with customers would then be reflective of that mindset or commitment.

The electric car company Tesla® operates with this MTP in mind: "Accelerate the transition to sustainable transportation." That's become a core component of the Tesla brand and every decision it makes. It guides and keeps everyone in the organization on the same path, establishing a clear vision for where the business is headed and what it must accomplish to get there. It tells everyone within the organization where to steer the Tesla ship. Through consistent messaging, it tells everyone outside the organization (you and me, for example) what it stands for and communicates that its brand is unique, memorable and changing the transportation landscape.

Let's get back to your business and your MTP—which is essentially a guidepost for your brand. Why does your business exist? What is its purpose? In his book *Start with Why*, Simon Sinek says people don't buy "what" you do. Instead, they buy "why" you do it. This is true for everyone your brand comes in contact with: you, your customers and, if applicable, your employees, shareholders and business partners. People care about why it is you're doing something. When they know where you're headed and what your overarching purpose is, they understand why it is you do one thing and not another. If you truly consider your "why," as you build your MTP, you'll be on your way to identifying what's most likely to motivate people to connect with your brand and your business.

And there definitely exists a "why," though you may have to dig to find it.

Focus on Your Purpose

You've been busy working at your craft. I get it. Yet, whether you're a cobbler, a brew master or a holistic healer, there's a reason you chose your given profession and launched it into a business. If you run a café, maybe you envisioned bringing people together so they could build strong connections over food. Maybe you wanted to help people lead more vibrant lives, making it easier to get healthy food on the go. Or maybe you wanted to infuse their day-to-day lives with some excitement, by introducing them to new flavor combinations. Your "why," like your individual vision for your business, will be distinct. Yet, it should reach beyond the question of profit to guide you toward the MTP that'll help your business connect with customers in a lasting way.

Let's bring the topic of purpose and its relationship to your business into clearer focus. Imagine there are two photography studios with differing whys. Photography Studio A's *why* is: "making people's most real selves shine through on camera." Photography Studio B's *why* is: "making people look their best in photos." Those working at Studio A might interview their clients before each photoshoot, having them fill out questionnaires or answer questions about their personalities and hobbies. This would help them figure out whether the subject is bubbly, serious, demure or more of a jokester. It then helps them encourage, highlight and capture those defining traits on film.

Knowing these insights and combining them with a driving *why* of having "people's best and real selves" appear on camera will affect how they approach camera angles, lighting and the overall shoot. Not so for those working at Studio B, who simply want to make people look their best in photos. For them, that could mean using high-tech lighting equipment and having a staff of hair and makeup people in-studio to prepare for and assist with the shoot. It could also mean lots of editing to photos after they have been shot. Rather than focus on their subjects' personalities, they might focus more on delivering technically-sound and flawless end products.

A great way to get to your *why* (albeit a bit morbid) is to consider how the eulogy for your brand might read. What was your brand like? Who had it touched? What problems did it solve? How did it impact the industry it was a part of? How did doing business with it make people feel? What did people think and say about your business? Write out what you hope people might say about your brand and its effects on them. This is a great exercise for defining your brand and getting clear about the power it holds.

Always, Could, Never

At Engineer Your Brand, when crafting MTPs, we use an "Always, Could, Never" approach.

This framework is a simple approach that's been used to help companies of all types define: What they'll *Always Be*, what they *Could Be* and what they'll *Never Be*. On a blank sheet of virtual or real paper, list everything that comes to mind, when you consider the current and future status of your business and brand, under three separate headers: Always Be, Could Be, Never Be. Include details related to:

- Your product or service offering
- Its attributes and benefits
- Your office/team culture

- Your location or reach
- Your business goals
- Your pricing or packaging

Include anything and everything you feel is important or influential to how your business will come to life.

That highly personal outline of what your brand will Always Be, what it Could Be and what it will Never Be gets you one step closer to creating the MTP which is powerful and true for you; one that's based on where you're at today and where you see yourself heading. Those two ingredients of where you are and where you're headed are key to building a purposeful statement you can own and promote with pride (via your brand). Based on that, try writing up a quick draft of your massive transformative purpose that your business stands for.

Once you have this statement written out, ask yourself if it could also apply to or make sense for another company either within your industry or outside of it. If it could also connect to another company, go back to the drawing board and align it more closely with your specific brand aspirations. Remember, when it comes to your brand, the goal is to make it uniquely yours. If nearly anyone could say what you're saying about your business, you may not be thinking BIG enough. You also run the risk of downplaying your own uniqueness. Your product or service is yours—no one else's. Own it. (You already do!)

If it helps, think back to the Tesla MTP: "Accelerate the transition to sustainable transportation." A company advancing solar power couldn't share this MTP with it. Nor could a car company that's looking to make "more renewable cars." Tesla doesn't specify how it will accomplish its MTP, since it could be done in several ways and may even been achieved utilizing technologies which don't exist today. It relies on these keywords: accelerate, transition, sustainable transportation. Those four words equal one strong MTP. Challenge yourself to limit your own word count!

By now, I hope you realize that this is where it begins—with your MTP, your mission statement or your statement of purpose. Whatever form it takes, from this point on, we'll create your brand around it. In the following chapters, we'll use your statement to engineer the way you and your stakeholders (i.e., consumers, employees, business partners) view your brand and, as a result, your business.

We'll not only use it to help you stay on track. We also use it to communicate who you are, explain what it is you stand for and position you—in the minds of others—as a take-charge, no-holds-barred business owner with a clear and unshakeable purpose. Doing that upfront will inspire you and those around you to achieve a purpose that goes beyond "selling more stuff." You'll amaze yourself, bringing your brand to life in meaningful ways which impact you daily.

Merely existing is now a thing of the past. Get ready to rock your brand!

Brand-Building Touchpoints:

- First, get clear about your "why."
- Then, establish your BIG brand purpose or MTP.
- Let that brand purpose propel your business forward.
- View it as a brand stamp or rallying cry others can get behind.
- Decide what your brand will Always Be, Could Be and will Never Be.

Your Brand Is Your Product or Service

What does your *offering* say about brand?

What sort of offering are you building your brand around? While your brand is the most important intangible aspect of your business, your product or service is the most tangible element of your brand. This is the "thing" people hold in their hands or minds. It's what lives on as a reminder of your interactions with them. They use it to satisfy a need, a want and even a desire. They may give it to someone else, as a gift. Precisely because this is often what people think of, when they think of your brand and what they actually exchanged money for, it's a key component in building your brand. So, it's critical to use your product or service to engineer the image of your brand that gets conjured up in people's minds.

Every detail of your product or service should be thoroughly thought out, as you build your brand. That's the only way to ensure that you leave the kind of lasting impression you want to be known for. Whether you put much thought into it or not, those details will serve as a reflection of your brand. That's why it's better to breathe life directly into those details and give your brand legs of its own. And, when I say detail, I mean every tiny, little detail. That includes everything from the screws you use to build your product and the suppliers you source raw materials from to how you lay out components and which features you build into your product or service offering.

All of it's important. While the thought of taking a micro-view approach may make you cringe, I promise, it'll be worth it! In the end, you'll craft an unmistakable brand that attracts your best possible customers—the kind you can't wait to do business with—like an array of paperclips to a supercharged magnet. In this chapter, we'll address those details one-by-one. That'll make the process less painful and more enjoyable.

Stand Out from the Crowd

What makes you, your product or your service different? Said differently, what qualities do you want to be known for? Your purpose will come in handy here: Why should customers choose you and how can you help them instantly recognize what distinguishes you and what you have to offer? When you set out to establish or reinvigorate your brand, these are important considerations. Take a hard look at the market you're in. Survey the websites and social media pages of business owners in the same sector.

What do you offer consumers which no one else can or chooses to offer? The list of distinctions can be wide-ranging, yet it's typically unique to your specific market or offering. For a food manufacturer, it could be a secret ingredient or a combination of uncommon ingredients that delivers a unique payoff in the form of flavor. For a furniture manufacturer, it could be a time-honored or patented process that results in the smoothest finishes; one your competitors shy away from either because it's cost-prohibitive for them or they simply aren't privy to it.

If you're a service provider, it could be that your business has a long history of being family-owned. Or, just maybe, you offer a unique service guarantee which no competitor offers or has the nerve to. If your bakery was initially opened by ancestors who brought great traditional recipes with them from one continent to another, play that up! The list truly is endless.

They key is figuring out what you do that's unique and then leveraging that to your advantage.

Let's stop a minute here. I see you scratching your head, saying, "What I do isn't that special." I beg to differ. Even if you believe that what you do or make isn't out of the ordinary, likely, there are people who routinely tell you otherwise. Think of new acquaintances who, when you tell them what you do, respond, "Wow! That's so cool." Think of customers who've written you notes or said, "I can't believe it. I absolutely love what you did!" The lesson here is that it pays to think about your business through the eyes of outsiders. While you may think it quite ordinary to import the ingredients you use in your French-inspired menu items directly from France, others find it an extraordinary feat. In their eyes, that also makes your dishes unique! Even if you are just starting out, and don't yet have these types of accolades, your business and brand are unique, you just need to see that for yourself.

That's the end goal: Find your own unique offering and using it to carve out a place for yourself in consumers' minds. For some products or services, I'll admit, the process might be more challenging. I mean, how different can one T-Shirt or food processor be from all the others? The key here is arriving at language that says what the others aren't saying and aligning your unusual way of expressing your brand and its benefits so that they're synonymous with your business.

For instance, imagine you own a juice company that specializes in serving healthy green beverages. All green juices contain more or less the same ingredients: spinach or kale, an apple, maybe celery, avocado and some sort of liquid base. Yes, there'll be numerous iterations on this drink recipe—but only so many ingredients give these drinks their vibrant green coloring. Essentially, both you and your competitors are selling health-inspired drinks full of green goodness. Your juices may even be made the exact same way: same ingredients, same preparation steps, same juicers used, etc. They may even taste the same. Yet, when it comes to naming, consumers begin to detect a level of differentiation and to form unique impressions of each brand available to them.

Your competitors have settled on Green Monster, Glowing Green, Mean Green and other variations along those lines, all of which bring up different images in themselves. While you may still want to use a green-themed name (more on naming later), what if your brand stood behind a secondary feature of your drink? It could be something that's also true for you competitors, except no one but you thought to call attention to it in an overt way. What if your brand took it upon itself to educate consumers about the fact that your green smoothie delivers 300% and 200% of their recommended daily intakes of Vitamin K and Vitamin A, respectively? By doing this, and explicitly calling this out, you cause consumers to consider how vitamin-dense your drink is and to second guess whether your competitors' green drinks are equally vitamin-rich. They know how much vitamin goodness they get from you but have no idea what anyone else offers, so they may as well pick your brand. With you they know they're getting 300% and 200% of Vitamins K and A. That has to be good, right? That's brand engineering!

Every other green juice in town may pack the same percentages of those nutrients. Yet, if no one promotes them in their messaging, consumers don't know they exist. If you're the only one making this claim public, consumers will view yours as being the only juice shop to offer this added benefit. The same principle applies if you own a restaurant and offer delivery service to your customers. Say you and all of your competitors guarantee delivery within 60 minutes or the order is free. You could be the only one to change how you word this statement. Instead of saying, "Under

60 minutes or it's free," you choose to say, smartly: "If it's not there in 60 minutes, we're buying you dinner!" You'd be saying the same thing. Only now you stand out in consumers' minds, by positioning your brand as one that cares so much that you treat them to free meals should something go wrong during the delivery process. It's a small tweak yes, but small tweaks make the world of a difference in branding.

I'm giving your imagination a workout, I know, but I can't state this enough: If you're struggling to identify something unique about your offerings, create a way of saying what others aren't saying that's unique to you. Building unique features and benefits into your products or services is always easier to do during the initial, development phase. Still, if you're in the process of rebranding your business, don't convince yourself that subtle or major changes are impossible. They can and must be made, if you hope to stand out from the crowd.

Other Ways to Be Unique

Another way of identifying traits which are unique to your business is to think about the features and benefits which are most important to your customers or end users. I like to classify these into two categories. The first category is comprised of things which are necessary to do business within your industry. Put another way, they're those features and benefits which must be included in your product or service for it to be competitive and/or function properly from a user standpoint. For example, if all your competitors claim to offer a complete meal in their packaged juice product, you will want to offer at minimum a complete meal as well since this is an expectation from your desired audience.

The second category is comprised of things which are entirely unique to your product, service or process. What can you do or offer that's 100%

uniquely yours? Or how could you modify your process—so that *your* customers benefit from the experience in a new and different way? There are things you think people need (because everyone else is offering them) and then there are features and benefits customers actually have a desire and/or a need for. These include things you claim ownership of already and things which have the potential to help you stand out in your area of specialization.

The earlier delivery service example is a good one to dissect according to mandatory needs and unique offerings. If you were to launch a delivery service, speed is something you'd absolutely have to make a priority and communicate as part of your offering. This is a need. No one wants their pizza delivered three hours from when they order it. When you consider a list of wants or unique offerings, however, you stumble on opportunities to evolve your brand in ways which are unique to you. Your twist on delivery could involve a bike, a drone or even white-glove service.

Each option builds a different brand image, so you'll want to weigh their potential pros and cons, in detail, before committing to a strategy and carrying it out. This is another area where paying attention to the tiniest details can benefit you in a number of ways. It's easy to think "fast delivery." After all, that may be a given in your industry. Building your brand comes into play when you begin thinking about how you'll get the word out ("If it's not there in 60 min., it's on us!") and how you'll follow through on your unique promise (i.e., by bike, by drone or by way of a silver platter).

Here's a way to drive that point home. Imagine having a pizza delivered to your home or office in one of three ways: 1.) by an impersonal high-tech drone, 2.) by a visually-impaired person who works for a nonprofit kitchen, or, 3.) by a bistro that offers white-glove service only. My guess is, each option resulted in a very different image of the brand behind your pizza delivery. Each one revealed something about your expectations for a particular brand and its respective mode of delivery. While, each one is a means of order fulfillment, they all give a unique spin to the traditional car/driver delivery service model. Beyond that we can all agree that they're three very different brands.

Have the floodgates opened yet? I hope so! It's my intent to get you thinking of at least a dozen different things you can say about your own product or service to make it unique—and of countless different features you can add to your product or service offering which will do the same. Being flooded with new ideas is a very good problem to have. Let all of them come through. Jot down anything you can say that would *wow* your consumer or separate you from your competition. Here are some prompts to get you started:

- How can you satisfy customer cravings?
- What can you say that no one else is saying?
- Which benefits/features can you add to the mix?
- How can you use wording to state things differently?
- How else can you differentiate your product or service?

List all of these claims out sans judgment, so you end up with an exhaustive list of unique claims, benefits and features your brand could own. Next, determine which elements are important to building connections with your own potential or existing customers. Focus on things consumers would want to get from a product or service like yours. Remember, you're in business to serve them. So, while you may think that your new manufacturing technology is the coolest thing around, you must ask yourself if this is (in fact) what consumers find truly important.

If your behind-the-scenes process doesn't do anything for the consumer or highlight some unique aspect of doing business with you (i.e., handcrafted, time-honored, 100% volunteer etc.), it doesn't need to factor into the conversation or your branding efforts. If the consumer doesn't know about something, it doesn't exist. Some of the claims you make or features you offer could be fantastic so don't get rid of them altogether. Just consider that they may not be what makes you unique in consumers' minds, which is why it's best to emphasize traits which will truly move the consumer to buy your product or service over a competitor's.

Take another look at the list of things you might say about your product or service and ask yourself:

- What have customers asked me for repeatedly?
- What sorts of things do they say they wish I offered?
- What should they know that no one else is talking about?
- What do they want a product to do that others don't/can't?
- What claims may comfort them, as they reach for their wallets?

Doing this will help you create another list. This one will help you take a deeper look at your business category and product or service offering through the eyes of your very best customers. Look for unique angles which will help you connect with them. Which of these items would move the dial in terms of separating you from the pack? Which of these features and/or benefits will help you build the brand you're looking to build? While you could deliver your products using a drone, think about whether that's the brand image you want to build for yourself. Is there a need for that service and does that decision serve the brand image you're looking to create?

If you believe customers are seeking a specific benefit, as a side effect of doing business with you, consider whether you can make it happen. Then, challenge yourself to turn that possibility into a reality—continuing down the path to creating a distinct and distinguishable brand.

People Expect Quality

Quality will almost always be something that remains at the forefront of people's minds when it comes to the products or services they buy. This becomes more and more important the more expensive your product or service is. Oftentimes you only get one chance to showcase your offerings, especially during a new product launch, so keep quality high on your list of priorities as you make related business decisions.

A good test for managing product quality is the Best Friend Test. As you touch your physical product or think about the service you offer, ask yourself if you could give it to your best friend with pride. That's not to say you need to have the absolute highest quality product out there. It's just that having a strong product you'd feel comfortable (if not great) giving to someone you care about is important to the longevity of your brand.

Quality can be derived from many things. The elements you choose to use and then call out in your branding efforts, if you call them out at all, will be important when building your unique brand. For example, you can build a higher quality product by using higher quality materials. Maybe instead of manufacturing the tables you sell out of oak, which is a common material, you decide to use walnut, which is stronger and less commonly used. This small change will create a different image of your brand than the images of those around you who opt for oak.

You can also improve the quality of your end product by: using an alternative manufacturing process, giving consumers a greater quantity of product than they'd get elsewhere or making sure your product is more environmentally-friendly than the competition's. Quality can also take the form of being made in a trusted location, while your competitors' products are made under less desirable conditions. Similarly, if everyone else is sourcing their parts from China, using American-made components may give you an edge and make customers feel as if they're getting a higher quality or more unique product with you.

Keep in consideration all the various parts of your product and how they relate to your brand. If you specialize in European desserts, each ingredient that goes into every delectable treat is important to the outcome. You want the results to taste exactly as you envisioned—and so do consumers! Knowing this, it's important to consider every single ingredient used in your recipe. It's also important to ask yourself whether it's needed, what its role is and whether there's a better ingredient which will do the same thing but can offer consumers an unexpected payoff. That something would help you stand out, as unique, within the space occupied by European desserts.

Let's say all sugars can be used interchangeably to give a dessert the same level of sweetness, yet certain sugars, like those derived from maple syrup have added health benefits like antioxidants, magnesium, and zinc. If you're trying to create a healthy dessert brand, using maple syrup rather than granulated sugar could be a great way to position your brand as a healthy dessert alternative. Similarly, if you're hoping to build a brand that celebrates national pride, it might be important for you to have every component of your brand made in the country you're building a connection to: America, Australia, Canada, Germany, China, wherever. Even if it's one small screw in a large mechanism that makes the end product you're selling more American, if you're building an American brand, use it. If you want your brand to truly symbolize American pride, stand behind that by using all-American parts. Even if the cost is slightly higher, the pay off you're likely to receive by being able to make bold brand claims will be worth it.

I once worked with a company that was trying to create the healthiest possible version of its food products. As part of this brand development, our team explored how we might do that from every conceivable angle. We determined that we could use the healthiest superfood ingredients available. We could also use the healthiest and most sustainable packaging options. We could call out the most compelling health claims. We were truly trying to create a go-to, healthy alternative in a category that was challenged and not well known for being healthy. In one of our upfront meetings, we explored every new possibility for creating this product—all the way down to having the product retain more of its overall nutritional value while going through the food manufacturing process.

Someone mentioned emerging technology similar to a microwave, which would allow our product to maintain higher levels of nutrition than our competitors' while also keeping the desired texture of the product. It wasn't a great idea, considering that we were looking to make our version healthier and that several years' worth of studies had led to the notion that microwaves and devices like them have a detrimental impact on people's overall health. This seemingly simple solution to maintaining nutrition was completely off-brand. It wasn't aligned with healthy eating and wouldn't have helped us create the type of product or brand we were hoping to. It simply didn't make sense from a brand consistency perspective. The moral here is: Even if something may help your product or service stand out in one way, make sure it remains true to brand in all other ways. Otherwise, you risk damaging your brand image altogether.

Your Brand's Sensory Impact

Another way to differentiate your brand is to think about which sensory experiences will help you make it more unique. Think about how your product looks, feels, tastes, smells and sounds. Obviously, not all of these are relevant to every industry, product or service. Simply focus on those which are important to your industry and then build out your brand (via your product or service experience) based on a variety of them, whenever possible.

If your product feels rough to the touch versus soft to the touch, it will align with a different set of associations with consumers. Leverage that difference! Play up a rough-textured product by creating a rugged brand image that's tough and durable. Play up a soft-textured product by creating a brand image that's delicate or gentle. If an item is heavy versus light, what brand images might come to mind? A heavy object will have an easier time carrying a brand image that's tailored around strength and durability than will a similar product weighing half as much.

What people see, feel, hear and smell has a profound impact on how they perceive and view the world around them. This is true for your own product or service offering. When working on the sensory elements of your brand, it's often best to work backward. First, get clear about the brand you want to create. Then, decide which sensory experiences will bring it to life. If you hope to create a masculine brand, how would the product feel to touch and then to carry? How would it look, smell, taste and sound? Chances are you won't wind up with a highly-scented, light and fluffy product.

While it's still difficult, building a masculine or feminine brand is sometimes easier than building a brand that's serious, intellectual or possesses feelings and traits which are otherwise wide open to interpretation. How does an intellectual product smell? How does a fun brand taste? How does a comforting brand sound? Even hugely successful brands have been asking themselves these questions for years and rightfully so. When building sensory experiences into your product or service, you're playing on a more primal and subconscious level than you are a conscious or obvious one.

Yet, affecting the subconscious leaves an imprint of your brand image in the consumer's mind. It does that more strongly than brands which don't make deep, sensory connections. Take, for example, a South Korea-based city bus campaign run by Dunkin' Donuts®, which combined a jingle with scent. As the Dunkin' Donuts jingle was played on select buses, the scent of fresh-brewed coffee was slowly released into the air. It was a nice, added advertising bonus some passengers consciously took note of while others didn't notice at all on the surface. What's impressive is the fact that, during the course of the campaign, visits to Dunkin' Donuts closest to bus stops along the route this campaign was run in increased by 16%. Further, sales at those same outlets rose by 29% compared to when the ads did not run.

Another example which shows how powerful sensory experiences can be to engineering an image of a brand is when BMW® decided to amplify the sporty feel of its 2014 M5 model. To plant the "sporty" seed in the minds of consumers, BMW designed its car so that an engine revving sound effect played through the car speakers, making the car sound and feel as if it had increased pep. Seemingly small details (which some brands put loads of time, energy and money behind) can do wonders to solidify an intended position in people's minds. It's time you started to think about how you can use sensory experiences, too, when designing or promoting your product or service.

What follows are a few questions to consider, as you explore the potential in each sensory area. Use these prompts to figure out how you can reinforce awareness of your product or service (and, therefore, brand) in people's minds. Note that—as human beings—sight is our most prominent sense, smell is most closely connected to emotion and taste is the most intimate of all.

Sight:

- What does it look like, overall?
- What colors are used?
- What shape is it?
- What size is it?
- Does it resemble anything of signifigance?

Sound:

- What does it sound like when in use?
- What does it sound like when not in use?
- What does opening the package sound like?
- What music is used to sell it and how loud is it?

Smell:

- What imagery is tied to its scent?
- What will its scent remind people of?
- What do companion products smell like?
- What scents compete with it, in selling situations?

Taste:

- How does it taste overall?
- How familiar or distinct is its taste?

- How does aftertaste affect user experience?
- How warming or cooling are its effects on taste?

Touch:
- What does it weigh?
- What is its texture like?
- What is its temperature?
- What do its materials feel like?

Your physical product is the most tangible element of your brand. If you're a service provider, you're the physical manifestation of your product. Regardless, your product is most likely what people will imagine when they think of, hear mention of or see your brand. Because of this, it's important to consider each and every detail your product embodies.

If you claim to have a healthy brand which can lead people to a more vibrant lifestyle, deliver on this healthy image in every way possible. Carefully think through and build out every element of your product design, presentation and communication strategies—so that they reinforce "health." This includes the ingredients you use, how they affect taste or texture, how the end product appears, which sounds are associated with it, how it smells and how it feels.

That and everything in between is critical to building a brand around your product or service.

Brand-Building Touchpoints:

- Build features and benefits into your product or service.
- Select those which consumers will find unique or compelling.
- If identifying what's unique is a challenge, identify distinct claims.
- Leverage product or service attributes no one else owns.
- Build sensory impact into your experience, branding at a primal level.

Your Brand Is Your Price

What does your *price* say about your brand?

Even if a $20 meal and a $200 meal are made exactly the same way, the $200 meal will always taste better. Why is that? Price establishes a baseline for what your brand is and what it represents. It does that by setting an expectation, in consumers' minds, as to: What type of product or service you offer, what sort of service or attention they can expect, what level of quality they will receive and how what they're purchasing from you stacks up within your industry. In the case of your $200 meal vs. your $20 meal, you expect that price equals quality, so you tell yourself the $200 meal tastes better as a result.

Your price and related pricing strategies, which we'll discuss in this chapter, also create a point of reference which distinguishes what you're selling from what someone else is selling. This one factor alone has the power to influence who your products and services speak to, allowing you to appeal to an entirely different customer base. That's because, whether we like to think it's true or not, brands are extensions of the people who buy them. People are attracted to and then purchase brands which they believe are reflective of themselves and the values they cherish.

The person who buys a Porsche® Boxster likely buys it because he or she believes those cars are peppy, sporty and rise to a level of luxury—as they themselves do or hope to. Of course, the functional benefits of extra horsepower and high-safety ratings will drive people to buy this car too, but let's not fool ourselves to think the image this vehicle carries doesn't also play a significant roll in the purchase decision. Those consumers are different from the ones who purchase Toyota® Corollas. Corolla owners pride themselves on being practical and straight-shooting, spending only what's necessary to get them from Point A to Point B as efficiently and effectively as possible. When you set a price for your own particular product or service, you're establishing a relationship with consumers; one in which the people who choose your business are attracted to what you're offering via language that reflects their values, albeit represented in numbers (i.e., price/cost to them) versus words (i.e., web content, ad copy).

Setting "the right price" is absolutely critical, when you're engineering your brand on purpose, since what people pay for what you offer alters what they think of you and whatever it is you're selling. There are three main pricing tiers which all offerings in a given market or industry fall into:

- *Economy* – lowest cost (offering the fewest frills)
- *Mass* – standard pricing (quality and benefits vary)
- *Premium* – highest cost option (noticeable benefits bundled in)

The three pricing tiers are very much as they sound. What varies between them, on the whole, is the extent of any features, services or benefits offered and expectations established through pricing. Selecting the right tier for your brand is dependent on four additional things:

- The "personal values" image you hope to project.
- The sorts of value-added perks you expect to offer.
- The margins you're working with or would like to achieve.
- The number of customers needed to reach your financial goals.

The price you charge for your brand is both relative to what you're offering and the brand image you're hoping to build. In order to clearly define your related pricing strategy, it helps to first gain an understanding of what others operating a business similar to yours are doing about pricing.

Other People's Prices

It's relatively easy to gain the perspective you need to price your own products or services well based on what the market is already willing to bear at all three pricing tiers. In that regard, other people's prices teach us an invaluable lesson. In particular, you need to get curious about knowing who offers the highest-priced alternatives and understanding how it is they can charge more than everyone else. Online or in-store research can reveal data on pricing at the local, regional, national and international levels. If you belong to an association which lists affiliates online, use its member search (or similar tool) as a starting point.

Type in your zip code and generate results for nearby businesses. They often include links to affiliate business websites, so visit the competitions' online stores. If pricing isn't posted there, use the "Contact Us" feature to request a price list. As you peruse their offerings, ask yourself a few questions. Do they offer some unique form of after-purchase care like an extended warranty or guarantee? Do they offer something that's unique to their product or service? It could be a special ingredient, a signature process or distinct packaging. Do they make claims no one else is making? Do they possess experience or expertise which is uncommon to your industry?

Ask yourself, too, whether they convey an image of quality and/or portray a lifestyle that might resonate with premium-level consumers. You'll know a premium product when you see it, as it's fairly easy to pick up on what makes it superior to the other offerings in the same category. There are many ways to justify a premium price. Those will be laid out later in this chapter. For now, it's enough to simply investigate what others are doing which is helping them set a price standard that affects all consumers within your category.

On the other end of the spectrum, you'll also want to know what shoppers' lowest-cost options are and what's being promised at that price point. Is the packaging, perhaps, less impressive? Are delivery terms strict, demonstrating a lack of urgency (i.e., "2 to 4 wks." for in-stock product)? Is quality lacking? Are service or support times longer than average (i.e., "within 72 hrs." versus same day or 24/7 live chat)? Life is full of trade-offs. Consumers are savvy enough to know that. Determine which trade-offs people are making, according to price paid, when it comes to the category you compete in.

With low-cost offerings, in particular, those trade-offs are oftentimes associated with things which aren't as critical to end users or consumers— which is why they feel comfortable following through with such transactions. If they can buy organic pet food from Whole Pet Foods at the lowest price and aren't pressed for time, they'll wait two weeks to receive it. However, if Fido's bowl is near empty, they'll pay a competitor who's willing to deliver it overnight a hefty upcharge on that same product.

Even if someone is struggling to make ends meet, there are times when he or she will pay more for a product or service. That is, when they're unwilling to make the perceived trade-off that comes with paying a lower price in the same category. This happens frequently at holidays and birthdays, when consumers rush to fill loved ones' wish lists. It also applies in situations which trigger the values consumers hold. Someone may be thrifty when it comes to clothing, because they don't see value in buying expensive clothes; however, that same person might regularly buy the most premium herbal supplement brand, because health is of the utmost importance to them.

Of course, you'll eventually want to understand what comes with mass price offerings. This is the category in which the most variance occurs, in terms of benefits and quality, and in which the greatest similarities exist between competitors. Some people in this price range will offer speedy service but no delightful packaging. Others may have delightful packaging but limit post-purchase service to "just the basics." Others still offer acceptable products or services, as far as consumers can tell, but have decided to offer their products at mid-tier because they don't deliver any of the bells or whistles associated with premium pricing. Yet, what they do offer goes beyond what low-cost providers are delivering and they know it.

By this point, you may be thinking: "What I offer is so similar to my competitors that no one will pay a premium price for it." Can you be sure? Is the most premium offering in your category really all that different from everyone else's, in terms of the functional benefits it provides? Or is it a case in which emotional benefits truly set it apart—and can you compete there? There are and will always be people who are happy to pay a premium price no matter how similar or different a product or service is, so take time to compare what's out there. The perceived value of what they get, in return for their dollars, embodies an air of prestige or luxury that's based on price and price alone. We're not talking comparison shoppers here. We're talking, "Top shelf, please!" When you truly understand your consumer and the real benefits they're after, both in life and from the products or services you offer, you'll come to know the power of creating a brand that truly connects with them.

Premium Pricing & You

If you're interested in charging a premium price for your product or service, find a way to offer consumers perks which extend beyond what they can easily find elsewhere. Zero in on what's truly of value to them and now you've positioned your brand as one that delivers BIG time! The added good news is that there are several ways you can justify premium pricing and make your product or service worth the extra expense. In general, people amendable to premium pricing expect high-quality products and service levels. The key differentiators which can then make you a major player in the premium pricing world are exceptional quality and exclusivity.

If you can't deliver one or (ideally) both, you won't be able to sustain a premium-price platform and should, instead, set your sights on mass or economy pricing. I'll outline both in a minute. First, let's explore exclusivity and quality. Exclusivity and quality are par for the course, when it comes to premium pricing, since products and services in this tier are priced out of reach for most people. If many would happily pay what you're charging and feel they got great value, in other words, you're a mass brand by nature. Premium brands stand out, go to great lengths to protect their trademarks and deliver well beyond standard expectations. All of that helps ensure that their products or services can't be easily duplicated.

Beyond establishing a sense of exclusivity or premier quality, there are a host of other things you can do to make your brand stand out for having premium associations. While your options may vary based on industry, here's a list of items to get you started along with examples of each:

- *Get certified.* – organic, fair trade, American-made, 100% recycled
- *Make it exclusive.* – limited edition, for new or existing customers

- *Price it accordingly.* – charge more for custom, specialty or limited runs
- *Emphasize higher quality.* – truffle oil, real leather, reclaimed hardwood
- *State your claim.* – fastest delivery, industry's best warranty, 24/7 support
- *Call attention to details.* – live-edge table, cold-pressed juice, hand-lettered
- *Highlight unique features.* – handcrafted, dermatologist-created, small batch
- *Capitalize on geography.* – locally-sourced ingredients, clients worldwide, Made in Paris
- *Make it function better.* – longest-wearing lipstick, multipurpose 3D printer

When considering whether you offer a premium service or are able to, think outside the box. If you ship product to people's homes, are you willing to add gift wrapping to your service options for an added fee? If you're a local grocer, can staff carry customers' purchases out to their cars for them? If you're a consultant, can you establish a practice of sending each of your clients a custom gift at the close of your contract? The goal is to make an impression no one else is making, by going above and beyond what's considered ordinary or standard.

Opting for Mass or Economy Pricing

The mass price point is relatively self-explanatory. In this range, your pricing is run of the mill when it comes to what's being offered in your selected industry or market. It is, therefore, sought out by the masses. This is where the majority of competitors fall, so you should expect to face a higher level of competition.

Consider the brand Nike®. While its shoes aren't cheap (averaging $149 a pair), they also aren't unattainable. Running shoes can range anywhere from $12 to $2,222. So, a price point of $149 makes Nikes seem attainable for the majority of people who want to own them. Rather than try to get on as many feet as possible, by offering them at a lower price, this brand makes an effort to get people's attention by creating an image of a lifestyle associated with its products. It connects with people on a values (vs. "value") level, communicated via the idea of chasing who you want to be and becoming your best self by simply going for it: *Just Do It.*

That one concept—coined, in 1988, in an ad agency meeting with Wieden+Kennedy—has proven to be highly-relatable and has positioned Nike as a worldwide leader in the mass category. The brand differentiates itself further through unique designs, add-on items and ancillary services (i.e., running classes, workout tips, sporting electronic partnerships), as well as by offering related lifestyle items, which range from athletic wear to shoelaces. Competitors who offer shoes at a similar price point have no trouble getting a sense for what they should also offer, in terms of quality and after-sale service.

Offering your own brand at mass price allows you to appeal to a wide range of potential customers, which is a good thing. Though, again, many will be competing in this tier. For that reason, it's still important to distinguish your brand as somewhat out of the ordinary. Taking cues from others regarding price doesn't mean you need to follow their lead when it comes to your offerings. If you choose to be comparable in terms of price, make sure to excel or stand out in some other way.

Economy pricing will allow you to be attainable among the greatest number of people. When it comes to building your brand, though, the question you must ask yourself is whether or not you want to appeal to everyone. In this price range, people most often make a decision to buy based on price alone. So, oftentimes, there's not much need for or space in which you can create a truly remarkable brand that actually stands out and connects with people. Yes, they'll have fewer expectations about what it is they'll receive with their purchases. Yet, if you hope consumers will become advocates for your brand, the road paved with lowered expectations doesn't necessarily lead to success. Sure, more people may be able to buy from you. But, if you reduce quality too much hoping to meet margin, you may end up with reviews like: "Well, you get what you pay for."

That's especially true if you deliver something that's not exactly what consumers wanted, needed or expected. Believe it or not, this is quite different from how someone would react if their expectations aren't fully met after you'd sold them either a mass or premium-priced offering. When those consumers' expectations aren't met, they are more likely to make concessions versus think poorly of your brand, product or company. So, while it sounds unfair, it's true: When it comes to pricing, perception speaks volumes. One of the great things about building a strong brand is that it keeps you from feeling as if you have to compete based on price alone.

While building a brand that has depth and character, you're simultaneously building an image that has life and connects with consumers on a deeper level—one that reaches past what it is they exchanged money for. The stronger your brand becomes the more money people are willing to pay for their own stake in it and the more forgiving they are should the experience be misaligned with their initial expectations and/or your ability to deliver on them. Having a strong brand identity in place also keeps you from feeling as if you have a need to compete based on pricing at all. Rather, it allows you to use price as a basis for engineering your ideas so that they sync up with the brand image you're looking to create and communicate.

What Will People Think?

By now you've figured out that how you price your products or services has an impact on what people think of your brand. It determines whether they feel special compared to everyone else, whether they feel as if they're on par with everyone else or whether they feel as if they got a better deal than everyone else. Expectations for fulfillment shift with each pricing tier and each tier has its own impact on brand image. To bring the notion of pricing and brand engineering to life, let's look at how Whole Foods Market® does business.

Whole Foods is considered a leader in the premium grocery shopping experience. Its shelves are lined with unique food items, most touting claims like: organic, free trade, handcrafted, limited availability, freshly made, etc. In addition to offering high-end or otherwise exclusive products, this grocer allows shoppers to grab fresh food on the go, have their purchases packaged in recycled paper bags and benefit from value-added services.

There's someone to bag your groceries, someone to carry them out to your car and someone willing to let you sample any product on its shelves. If you want to buy a cup of coffee or sit down for a glass of wine and a quality meal while you're there? You can do that, too! Whole Foods customers happily pay premium prices—as an anticipated trade-off—to receive the exclusive benefits being a Whole Foods shopper affords them. Thus, they exit the store feeling as if they've purchased products of the highest quality. Along with herbal toothpaste and natural peanut butter, that's exactly what its clientele is in the market for.

Conversely, Walmart® prides itself on offering the absolute lowest prices on everything that lines its shelves. Its name is synonymous with low prices and its commitment is so strong that the company will price match any item a competitor's flyer shows is currently being offered at a lower price. While it does also stock organic items and products making premium claims, that isn't what people think of when they think of Walmart. Instead, they imagine a no-frills shopping environment. People aren't stopping to get a glass of wine midway through their rounds. They aren't requesting samples of aged cheddar cheese or nibbling on freshly baked croissants. They expect to find mainstream brands represented, are willing to overlook mediocre displays and, most importantly, want to pay as little as possible for a wide range of products.

At Walmart—just as you would at Whole Foods—you'll find people who are willing to pay for the sort of brand, inherent trade-offs and values they hold dear. What they both teach us is this: Your brand can live and thrive at the premium, mass or economy tier. What's important is that your brand delivers on the expectations people associate with the prices you charge and that your brand remains aligned with that pricing tier. As I shop in Whole Foods, I don't expect to wait in long lines nor to be subjected to ongoing messages conveyed over the store's public address system. Similarly, as I shop in Walmart, I don't expect an employee to stop what they're doing so they can help me sample an intriguing jam I might consider buying, if I like it well enough.

Just the same, if your own product or service is built on attributes like premium, unique or one-of-a-kind and yet I pay a low price for it, I'm not going to believe any of the claims you've worked so hard to make me believe. Your product or service and the price you charge for it must be aligned or you risk compromising consumer trust. A lack of trust never results in long-term relationships between consumers and vendors, whatever your price point may be.

Stay True to Your Pricing Strategy

That last warning dovetails nicely into one final bit of advice, when it comes to pricing. Promotions are just as important as everyday pricing when you're engineering your brand, so stay true to your chosen strategy. Do this even when you offer special promotions or sale items. Why? Doing so demonstrates brand integrity, sends a message that's true to brand and reinforces the values consumers have come to believe you stand behind.

When you initially set your prices and begin to shape your brand, consider any promotions you might offer later and how they will affect your ability to stay true to your selected price category. Let's say your prices are consistently in line with the top-third of all sellers in your market or industry. Be sure that any promotions you offer still fall within this price range. The same rule applies to the degree of any discounts you offer, as well as how often you discount products or services which fall under your brand banner.

Think of the brand Apple®. Its products rarely go on sale. If Apple does have a sale, any discount it offers is minimal, usually only 10%. Does this deter people from buying its products? Absolutely not. People are still happy to wait in lines which run around the corner and then pay full price for the company's products, doing so as frequently as each new release is announced. Apple has created a premium brand image and has stayed true to this, by not discounting its products, thereby avoiding any interruption in the premium brand image sway it holds in consumers' minds. Its premium pricing strategy reinforces its premium brand image.

Maintaining a brand image that's consistent is so many times overlooked. When we feel a need to drive immediate sales into our businesses, oftentimes we forget to consider whether deviating from a given strategy would do more harm than good. Well, I'm here to tell you: It *will* do your brand more harm than good. Always stick with your chosen strategy. Resist the temptation to go off-brand simply because you want to run a promotion or fill your showroom with a large number of potential customers. If you've worked hard to create a premium brand, offering "60% Off" once a quarter does nothing but attract customers who want your products or services at 60% off and are willing to wait until the quarterly sale hits to make a purchase.

I take that back. It does do something else. It drives *away* customers who are interested in and willing to pay more for an exclusive, high-quality shopping experience with you. In essence, it erodes your brand so that people think less of it and are less willing to pay a premium price for it. This has the added negative side effect of making it seem as if you need to reduce your prices more often, setting off a vicious cycle which may find you convincing yourself that this is a crucial sales period for you. Don't believe that line of faulty thinking. If you have something premium to offer and people are willing to pay a premium price for it, your job becomes attracting more of those consumers and steering clear of people who don't see the value in what you offer. Stay true to your brand and you will succeed.

Building your brand through pricing isn't limited only by what you charge or what sort of discounts are involved. It also includes the types of payment options you offer. Making it easy for customers to pay you in a variety of ways is another means for differentiating how you position your brand. For instance, is PayPal an online option that appeals to your customers? Is Bitcoin something that appeals to them? Would bartering—or an exchange of services—be useful? Take these things into consideration, as they relate to the unique brand image you're creating.

If they're in line with your brand, implement them. If they're not, avoid them. Like any other branding task, consider your consumer first. If a new payment option would benefit both you and your customer, go for it. If not, think twice. If your ideal consumer is the tech-savvy, cutting-edge developer who would rave about the fact that you accept payment by Bitcoin or your own proprietary form of cryptocurrency. Consider it. If your brand is built on an economy of sharing, maybe allow someone to donate their time and help you with a task in exchange for products or services. In these and other ways, examine what makes sense for your consumer and your brand. Your payment methods must make sense. Just because one client is tech-savvy and uses Bitcoin doesn't mean that's relevant to how you want to build your brand. The questions you must ask is what payment option do they want when buying your product or service.

What's the bottom line here? Pricing sets the tone for what people expect from your brand. There are countless ways to sell $1,000,000 worth of anything. You can sell 2,000 people something at $500 each, 1,000 people something at $1,000 each or 100 people something at $10,000 each. You can even sell 100,000 people something at $10 each. Choose the winning combination for your brand, making sure it's aligned with the value you offer people. What matters is that you think about the purpose behind your brand and then arrive at the right pricing strategy from there. People expect different things at different price points. If you don't deliver on those expectations, you've confused your consumer. That's not something you want to do. You want to ensure that everything your brand does projects a consistent image of what your brand is, what it stands for and what it offers people.

Stay true to your pricing strategy and you'll have no problem staying true to your brand.

Brand-Building Touchpoints:

- There are 3 main pricing categories: Premium, Mass, Economy.
- Each price tier positions your product/service differently, so choose wisely.
- Stay true to your pricing tier, even when offering special promotions or sales.

Your Brand Is Where People Find You

What does your *location* say about your brand?

Where would you like people to be able to purchase what it is you're selling? When you consider location, it's helpful to think of an actual shopper or customer you serve. Visualize this person on the hunt to solve a problem that you provide a solution for. Where might they be looking? What types of stores would this person be shopping in? Would they be in stores at all? People shop at discount stores for certain items, yes, but do you want your brand to have a discount store feel to it?

Would a better fit for your ideal customer be an online experience? A high-end retail shop? A specialty store? A spa or pharmacy? If you offer a service, you should think about where your office might be located or whether people expect you to serve them in group settings or in one-on-one situations only. Your answers are important and can help you engineer your brand on a whole new level. If you're a food manufacturer, can customers find your products in every major grocery store or only in local or boutique grocery chains? Maybe they won't find your products in stores at all, since you sell them exclusively via the trendiest farmers' markets.

Perhaps they can only buy your products online via your own website or an affiliate's website. Decisions about where your products are sold matter, when it comes to building your brand, yet placement also shapes your brand image. You may not always be able to control where your brand is displayed, when you're selling it through someone else. Hopefully, though, being equipped with the information in this chapter will enable you to understand why you should *push* to receive the best placement you can—maintaining at least some control over your brand.

Location & Perception

Where people "find you" shapes what they think of your brand. Outside of a few select industries, there are countless locations in which people can purchase a full range of products or services. To get you thinking about the various channels or outlets available to you, here's a quick list of different store types a clothing or accessory brand might align its products with:

- Its own personally branded store, website or pop-up location
- "Big Box" Stores (i.e., Forever 21®, Nordstrom®, Walmart)
- Stores selling closely related products (i.e., hats, shoes)
- Stores selling entirely different products (i.e., hair care)
- Boutique, hobby, museum or other specialty shops
- Third-party websites (i.e., Amazon®, eBay®)
- Brick and mortar or online discounters
- Drug stores or convenience stores

That's a wide array. Your goal is to first imagine all of the places your customer might visit through the course of a day, week, month or year. Then, whittle that list down to those places in which they'd be of the mindset to buy what it is you're selling. If your brand stands for ultimate convenience, absolute musts for your placement strategy include making sure your products or services are advertised on as many websites as possible, available for immediate purchase and, if applicable, shipped directly or quickly to the consumer. If, however, you're building a brand that's exclusive and intended for a narrow target audience, maybe sell only via your own store and/or website. The latter also gives you the opportunity to elaborate on your brand mission and values.

You can also engineer the perception of your brand by being sold in locations which are aligned with your brand image but are less expected. Let's say the clothing or accessory manufacturer mentioned earlier is trying to create a lifestyle brand for young, trendy people who live in a metropolitan city. Their brand engineering strategy might involve having their brand sold in a coffee shop which appeals to the same audience and is building a similar lifestyle image. Selling a brand this way helps you differentiate yourself, by: creating a footprint off the well-beaten competitor path, allowing you to own this unique purchase opportunity and building your brand image in association with a noncompeting but complementary brand. As long as that coffee shop's brand identity is a positive one and is aligned with the image you're looking to promote, this strategy can work wonderfully for any brand in any category.

Once you've identified a list of places it makes sense to align your brand with, review your list again and determine which channels are mandatory for you—even if those partnerships won't generate a high volume of sales. Remember, building your brand (aka your most valuable asset) takes time. Not everything you will do will result in immediate or abundant sales. This is a long-term game and you have to stick with it to win.

When Vitaminwater® was first launched in Canada, I was part of the team tasked with building out the brand through distribution efforts. The brand, which sells flavored water enhanced with different vitamin combinations, had already achieved celebrity status in the U.S. It was now intent on creating a similarly high-end, or premium, feel when it launched in Canada.

Knowing this, our team's goal was to get the product distributed in any and all stores possible within the postal code areas where its target audience lived or shopped: boutique grocery stores, clothing stores, boating stores, hiking stores and literally anywhere else those consumers might be. The aim was to make members of this specific target audience (and only this target audience) feel as if Vitaminwater was everywhere they went. As the brand established itself, distribution was opened up to any location that would carry it, but this was only after the exclusivity of the brand had been established. At the onset, it was critical that the brand only be available to its target audience—resulting in an exclusive, selective feel that endured.

Another example is the skincare company that's trying to position itself as a trusted, high-quality, dermatologist-recommended brand. To create this image, the skincare company would be wise to secure distribution in spas versus traditional drug stores where mainstream skincare brands are sold. People who visit spas arrive at those locations with skincare top of mind. Improving the appearance of their skin is something they're already investing in and are willing to spend money on. Devise a similar strategy of your own brand. Identify establishments with images similar to yours (ones which attract the kind of consumers you're hoping to connect with) and work at getting distribution with them, building up your brand image and customer base that way.

Product Placement

Once you've determined where your products will be sold, determine where they'll be positioned or placed within that venue. Let's assume your brand is being sold in a grocery store. Ideally, where in the store would you like your goods to be located? Having your products stocked alongside competitors' products may be an obvious selection and may be where you need to be, since that's where people will first look to have the specific need you solve met. The retailer might even force your products into that particular section of the store. Yet, think. Are there other areas of the grocery store where it also makes sense for your brand to be located? Are there opportunities to build your brand in association with companion products? If you make a delectable four-berry jam in small batches using locally-sourced ingredients, what regional food items do they pair nicely with? Push for placement alongside them, in addition to being placed next to the other jams in the store.

Say you're selling a stain-removing product in a grocery store that's building its own brand image around reliability. Reinforce to the retailer that your product is reliable at removing even the toughest stains: red wine, grape juice, spaghetti sauce, crayon marks. Building this brand image for your own product, as well as for the store's benefit, might open up placement where each of those items are sold. Not to mention where frozen berries, bulk coffee and tea are sold. While you may not be able to get placement in all of those locations all of the time, it's worth having a conversation about it.

Multiple placements help build up your brand, reinforce what it does and sell more products to those in search (or eventual need) of a stain-removing solution or whatever it is you are selling. You can do this online, as well. Work with web-based outlets which carry your stain remover to find ways your product can pop up as a special "Bonus!" buy item when consumers buy stain-producing culprits. This is a win-win, as it not only serves to build your brand but boosts overall sales for the retailer. Unless you're selling out of your own store, you will need to push for these additional placements. It's possible you'll be asked to pay for such placement, but that investment has the potential to increase sales and consumer awareness of the brand you're working so hard to build.

You Need to Be Online

According to U.S. Census Bureau reports for Q4 2017, sales from online stores accounted for nearly 10% of all U.S. sales. Online sales figures continue to grow each year and show no signs of slowing down. People buy everything from appliances and clothing to cars and groceries online. This behavior has become commonplace for shoppers in all sorts of industries. Does that mean you should absolutely have a presence online?

If you think your consumer would benefit from being able to buy your offerings online and you believe you can control their brand experience, yes. Given the growth potential with online sales, I encourage you to find a way to sell online so you don't miss out on these important selling opportunities. For example, if you own and run a luxury shoe brand, find a way to sell your specialty shoes to consumers who like to browse the web. Just be sure their entire online experience with you—from browsing to delivery and potential returns—screams, "Luxury!"

That's what the carmaker Tesla did, initially forcing consumers to its website to purchase its cars online at $100,000 USD and up. It was the only auto manufacturer to sell new cars online (luxury cars at that) directly to consumers. This made the process easier on consumers and modernized the entire car-buying process. People could still view Tesla vehicles at auto shows and at events where target audience members were known to gather, yet there wasn't one Tesla auto dealership you could drive up to or request a test drive from. The online purchase process, however, got people excited to buy this futuristic electric vehicle. Once a car was ready to ship, it was hand-delivered directly to the individual at whatever location they designated. The delivery process was meant to be a flashy spectacle, creating a luxe image for both the Tesla brand and the consumer. It was a purchase experience unlike any the auto industry had ever seen or taken part in.

So, don't feel as if you need to set up shop where or how others have done so previously. Think about what makes sense for your brand. Maybe it doesn't make sense to be where everyone else is. Maybe that's not what your brand is about. Take Casper® mattresses, a brand promising that nothing would come between you and a great night's sleep. The company created a young, transparent, accessible brand for unconventional mattress shoppers. Realizing that selling its mattresses in traditional sleep stores or department stores wouldn't make sense for its brand, it instead decided to ship directly to consumers' homes. Many would have said the idea was ridiculous—even though an awkward, 3-minute recline on a mattress in a store doesn't do much in terms of letting you test out a mattress, does it?

Not only did the strategy work; it revolutionized the entire mattress category. There are now countless direct-to-home mattresses available for sale online. The category was ripe for change. By challenging the convention that a mattress needed to be laid on before it was purchased, Casper created a placement strategy of its own: Ship directly to consumers and include a "100 Night" sleep-trial guarantee to make purchasing easier and to reduce the risk people might experience at not being able to try before they buy. This resulted in a strong, relevant brand which leveraged unique placement to drive home a core concept that shook up an entire industry and helped it connect with like-minded mattress shoppers.

After the company's 2014 launch, it held true to exclusively selling mattresses online until 2017. The majority of its mattresses are still discovered and purchased online, though consumers can also turn to a few on-brand stores (like Target) to get a firsthand glimpse at Casper products.

In addition, they can test them out in various pop-up locations around major cities.

A Quick Geography Lesson

What geographic markets make the most sense for your products and services? Deciding which regions or countries your brand reaches will help shape its image now and into the future. You might opt to promote it across the U.S. or concentrate your efforts in New York and Los Angeles only. Maybe your particular brand will live in one city, especially if it's a restaurant looking to impress local residents with diverse food offerings. Maybe it'll be available on every continent like Coca-Cola and Apple are. What's right for your brand depends on the goals and vision you hold for your company and may change with time. So, while location matters, resist putting hard and fast boundaries around where people find your brand. But do follow a few basic guidelines.

If your brand is regional, it may not connect with people outside of your area. In that case, don't worry about going national unless elements of your brand are adaptable for a wider market. A refrigerator brand that emphasizes its ice-making feature won't be as relevant to folks in Toronto, Ontario, who endure wind and snow half of the year, as it would be to people in Austin, Texas, who enjoy hotter climates year round and have a need for ice in home all year long. If you hope your brand finds a home in several cities, states and/or nations, adjust its features and messaging just enough to connect with people in different markets.

Coca-Cola has a presence in every country around the world. How it markets itself in each region differs slightly, while it remains true to brand and purpose. If Coca-Cola stands for youthfulness, it's no surprise that this concept has different meanings in different markets. What represents youthful happiness in the U.S. differs from what consumers associate with the concept in Spain or Japan. Cultural differences necessitate that your brand be tweaked slightly to make sense for where you'll have a presence. In the U.S., youthfulness might be represented through an image of wholesome teens laughing around a bonfire. In Europe, it might be conveyed by an image of teens dancing at an outdoor concert. In Japan? Two people giggling gleefully in a park. One size does not fit all, when it comes to expressing ideas aimed at different locations and different cultures.

The location of your brand (whether brick-and-mortar, online or both) determines the location your brand occupies in consumers' minds. You must be where your consumers are, in locations which make sense for the brand image you're building. That's true whether we're talking about the types of stores your products are found in, the geographic regions you operate out of or the placement terms you negotiate. All of these decisions will shape your brand and what people believe it stands for. Choose wisely, as to where your brand will be located, and also remember that where you are right now doesn't mean that's where you'll always need to be or *should* be. As consumers evolve and your brand grows its connections with them, you may just find that you're closer and closer to being exactly where your consumers want to be.

Brand-Building Touchpoints:

- Expand your reach, being sold by others who have similar brand values.
- Consider consumer needs, letting that dictate how or where you sell.
- Use untraditional placement to increase your brand presence.
- Sell where it makes sense for your brand and its consumers.

Your Brand Is Your Packaging

What does your *packaging* say about your brand?

First impressions matter. When it comes to branding your business, it pays to remember this adage. If you're selling a physical product, the packaging it's wrapped in ends up making an impression people will continue to associate with your brand. If you're selling a service, your website and marketing materials do the same for you. Everything from design to materials used, texture and shape—all the way down to the act of opening up that package or landing on your website homepage—serve as a reflection of your unique brand. Each of these elements presents you with an opportunity to convey your brand purpose and meaning long before a consumer interacts with you or even buys from you. While this chapter focuses primarily on physical packaging, it's also sprinkled with suggestions of benefit to service providers.

Packaging is an extremely important element of your brand, yet rarely is it given the time it deserves in the brand-building process. Like every other aspect of building your brand, each little detail should be reviewed and decided on to ensure that it's true to the brand you're building. Yes, even the tiniest of materials you use to build your product should be taken into consideration. Think about your target audience for a moment. Imagine them holding your product in their hands. If you're a graphic designer, image them holding a physical copy of a brochure you designed for them. If you're a consultant, image them holding a quote for service you wrote on their behalf. Then ask yourself:

- How do I want this customer of mine to feel?
- What obstacles do/did I intend to help them overcome?
- What images do I want to plant, in their minds, about my brand?
- Is that communicated in their interactions with me or my product(s)?

If you sell a vegan toothpaste, for instance, an important image to convey may be that you own and operate a conscious brand which cares about its consumers and the planet. Since you have a need to express that the environment is important to you, it's wise to use packaging materials that are eco-friendly, recyclable, biodegradable and/or can be repurposed after use via upcycling. While consumers may be originally drawn to your product because of your vegan claim, with this comes an underlying expectation of what your brand stands for. If you want to help consumers truly connect with you and to then turn them into advocates, you must take into consideration what else goes into building your brand image in consumers' minds.

There is a wide range of packaging materials to choose from. Each choice creates a different brand impression, making it easy to view packaging as an opportunity to build your brand before people lay their hands on your product. To get you started, here are a few ways to differentiate your packaging:

- *Texture* – soft, delicate, durable, malleable
- *Appearance* – transparent, matte, high gloss, no frills, luxe
- *Materials* – eco-friendly, low cost, minimalist, exotic, premium
- *Origins* – handcrafted, locally-sourced, Made in the hills of Switzerland

Each choice unconsciously creates a distinct brand image in consumers' minds. The look, feel and even smell associated with each impression contribute to their image of your brand. In turn, the materials used should align with the image you're engineering. If you want your brand to be known for ruggedness and durability, the materials used in your product packaging should reflect this. While that concept may seem simple enough, you may find that durable packaging costs three times more than any number of less durable, more affordable options. This is what oftentimes leads brands to veer off course, though there's a price to be paid for pinching pennies at every turn.

In a situation like that one, how do you communicate durability while maintaining reasonable prices and keeping production costs low? Think back to prior chapters: There are many ways to deliver and remain true to brand. Perhaps you initially hoped to present your crushproof travel mug in a tin case, taking the engineered idea of durability to the next level. Yet, it was cost-prohibitive. You could just as easily consider having its case constructed from wood, heavy-duty cardboard or sturdy plastic. While there are many ways to build your brand through choice of materials, you'll likely be faced with striking a balance between cost and brand impact. Achieve the right balance without sacrificing the image you're creating for your audience. What follows are a number of options for maximizing your packaging's impact.

Use Shape & Form to Stand Out

Are you making the most of your product or it's packaging, by using shape to communicate something new and exciting about your brand? If not, think of ways you can do just that. Shape can give visible form to your ideas and bring your particular brand to life. What you deliver doesn't need to conform to the shapes being used by your competitors. If it does, do what you can to resist industry norms and to make a name for yourself. The best shape for your brand should be dictated by something larger: your purpose, your customers' needs and the image you hold for your brand in its current state and in the future.

Don't follow the herd, if it steers you off course from creating your unique brand image in consumers' minds. Let's say your company produces cereal. Does your packaging truly need to fit within the confines of a rectangular box that's the same dimensions as everyone else's? Perhaps it can be shorter, wider or even packaged without a box at all. A bag may be all that's needed. Consider, too, whether your packaging will be cherished—as part of the brand experience—or whether it will be disposed of right away.

Nature's Path® cereal is an independent, certified-organic, wholesome brand that promotes itself as being both responsible and vested in doing what's right for consumers and the planet. Given its brand promise of being responsible for its contributions, it did away with the outer cardboard box for most of its cereal products. That wasted cardboard resulted in unnecessary packaging which ran counter to its all-around, environmentally-friendly brand. The result is a simple, matte bag that has everything you'd find on a box printed directly on it. This delivers on the company's brand promise and allows it to noticeably stand out on supermarket shelves.

When considering the shape of your own product packaging, know that where and how what you offer is sold should play a role in determining your options. If it will be sold in a retail store, imagine customers carrying it to checkout, having it bagged up with their other items and then transporting it home. I once worked with a company wherein the team tasked with managing a new product launch failed to take into account how the item would be displayed on grocery store shelves.

In a category where most of its competitors' products were packaged in a box, this product was packaged in a bag. While this was a fantastic way to stand out on shelves, the product failed to stand upright on its own. As a result of the oversight, it couldn't be properly displayed in stores without toppling over. People who were shopping couldn't locate the product, even when they were standing right in front of it. It made retailers' shelves look messy and the product itself looked sloppy, since the bag it was in kept slumping over sideways. Clearly, it didn't look its best. When it came to first impressions, this product failed to make a positive and lasting one.

Inspire a Sense of Delight

Let's talk about what *will* help you make a positive, lasting impression. Inspiring a sense of delight gets consumers excited to do business with you. So, think: How can I delight people with interesting packaging or as they open up my product? When they unbox the contents, is the experience an easy one? It should be. Does it lead to excitement? Frustration? Or, worse still: a letdown? Opening or unboxing your product should be a seamless process that avoids leaving the consumer to fumble around while opening it. It should reinforce your brand message, while being simple and enjoyable.

One way you achieve that is to use brand-building copy along the way. Let's assume you sell a handcrafted, honey-and-pear-scented soy candle that's delivered in a small box. When consumers open one flap of that package, perhaps a message about the handcrafted procedure appears. When they open the next flap, they see another message. This one talks about the benefits of using a soy-based candle. Finally, the last flap (the one separating the consumer from their candle) describes the comforting and alluring natural scents they're about to experience thanks to this delightful candle. The consumer has been brought into the brand story, through your packaging, and is delighted and excited before the first flame is ever lit. This is a powerful way to instill a positive array of feelings and emotions in consumers who, in turn, become brand advocates for you.

That's the key here. You can do tiny things to alter your packaging, like putting brand-building copy on a flap or removing a box—literally, a barrier to what's inside—altogether. These little touches can do wonders, when it comes to engineering and building a brand consumers fall in love with. Take every available opportunity to both build your brand and build a connection with consumers. On your part, the most it requires is a bit of creative role play (so that you can view your product through the eyes of end users) and a bit of thinking, well, outside the box!

I once worked on the brand development for a direct-to-consumer mattress firm that did a great job of making the most of its "unboxing" experience. The parent company, like all other direct-to-consumer mattress companies in this category, shipped its mattresses coiled up tightly in durable plastic and then stuffed into large, rectangular boxes destined for consumers' doorsteps. Once a box was opened, the tightly-wrapped bundle was removed, the plastic was cut away from it and the product was laid out, the mattress would expand to full size right before the consumer's eyes.

Rather than creating an extra step for the consumer, by having them go grab a pair of scissors and cut through the plastic (gently, now, so as not to ruin the mattress itself), this company opted to include in its packaging a handheld plastic cutter with its company logo imprinted on it. The device was designed to cut through the plastic perfectly and in a delicate manner. It was easy and extremely satisfying to use, allowing people to get to their mattresses sooner and safer than before. Consumers loved getting in on the fun as much as they loved watching their mattresses expand in size. This small plastic cutter, when bundled in with the product, made the entire unboxing experience more enjoyable and led to more positive associations with the brand, as a whole. It was an inspired act of branding magic.

What can you do to make getting to your product easier? Are there adjustments you can make, in regard to package functioning, which will make the experience more exciting and your brand more memorable for customers? Envision your product being opened and closed. Consider whether it needs to be resealed at some point. How can you make opening and closing it on a regular basis even easier? If the consumer isn't likely to use all of the product in one sitting, is there a way to preserve its quality until it's used again?

If you're a service provider, is there a way to change up your website landing page or YouTube tutorial videos so that customers have reason to keep coming back for more? What new and exciting information can you offer, in the form of an email campaign or downloadable tip sheets, which will make you stand out as a market leader? Whatever your specialty, find a way to make consumers' lives easier so that they enjoy interacting with your brand—from first use to last use. You'll be surprised by how favorably they respond.

Choose Language That Captivates

Language provides you with a way to captivate your audience. Every word that appears on your packaging (or, for service providers, in your online and print materials) should be carefully thought out so that it brings your brand to life. A full chapter in this book is dedicated to writing copy, but some important notes related to packaging are shared here. Every single brand can benefit from a short description which explains what consumers are about to buy from you. This should appear on your packaging. If you're a service provider, add it to the signature line of your emails.

Resist explaining the functional aspects of contents themselves. That's a wasted opportunity, since people will already know what it is they're buying from you. Let's say you're selling natural shampoo. There's no need to repeat "natural shampoo, natural shampoo" multiple times in your packaging copy, though you will want to do this when writing copy for your website (so that it's highly searchable). Instead, utilize that space to emphasize the emotional benefits your brand offers consumers. Does your natural shampoo make them feel more connected to the planet or more secure about what touches their bodies? Does it make them happier, knowing their life routines can be aligned with their values? Emotions play a larger role in helping consumers determine whether your brand reflects their values better than someone else's might.

Let's say your package is a beautiful glass container boasting some of Canada's best maple syrup for sale. Rather than simply labeling the packaging "Maple Syrup," or even "Pure Maple Syrup," you could touch on aspects of the product which encourage consumers to imagine using and enjoying it. The words "the purest maple syrup from the heart of Quebec" make it easy to picture a winter wonderland and the quintessential Canadian experience. Or, it may be worth mentioning that the package contains "maple syrup good enough for grandma's pancakes." This results in a flood of memories, ideas and emotions associated with comfort food and with time spent at grandma's house. A few, simple words of copy on your packaging can turn your brand from one that's merely functional into one that elicits an endearing, emotional response.

Yet, don't stop there. All of the copy you use on your package should bring your brand to life in ways which are vivid and memorable. This is done extremely well for every variety of the vitamin-enhanced, flavored-water beverage brand Vitaminwater. A peek at the copy used on any one of its bottles reveals great product packaging which literally brings the brand to life. The color and copy on the front label for each flavor has its own unique flair but is similar enough to the others, in tone and character, to remain true to brand. Its packaging copy reveals the brand's light-hearted, fun-loving and cheeky nature. While not taking itself too seriously, the brand also describes the exact ingredients of each drink and outlines how each recipe benefits consumers.

When deciding which flavor to buy, people refer to the distinct name assigned to each one: Energy, Focus, Power-C, Restore, etc. They might then read the vitamin combinations and skim the additional copy to get a sense for what the brand is all about. Playful sayings—like, "Tastes better than a screensaver of a tropical island looks!" (Tropical Mango) and, "Hello, taste buds. Welcome back to the land of the living." (Revive)—bring the brand's individual flavors to life even more, while explaining what each product aims to deliver for the consumer.

It's highly common for people to choose specific flavors based on the copy which appears on related packaging or to choose based on which flavor "speaks to them" and their vision of themselves, in that moment or on the whole. The packaging copy, specific bottle shape and label design of this product line are all crucial elements in making Vitaminwater, well, Vitaminwater.

If your own product packaging features instructions, consider writing them in a way that builds your brand. If nutritional tables or ingredient lists also appear on your packaging, use those as additional brand-building tools.

Rather than say, "Vitamin C", perhaps you can say, "Vitamin C—to keep you healthy!" Don't stop at, "Open here," when you can send the message, "Open happiness here!" Every word is an opportunity. Have some fun and let what you say about your brand build excitement and create positive expectations for what awaits consumers.

Don't forget your barcode, either. If it makes sense for your brand, use it to build and strengthen your brand image. These little surprises create moments of delight for consumers and go a long way toward giving outward expression to your brand. Some companies have gone to great lengths to incorporate their brands into their barcodes, making them an integral part of their overall package design. They've done this in clever ways which have strengthened their holds within their respective markets and reinforced the images they wish to portray publicly. See the unique and different barcodes below and think what could you do to bring your brand to life through this otherwise functional aspect of the package.

What about technology? Should it play a role in your packaging? If you're building a brand that's based on technology, find ways to allow your packaging to bring that expertise to life for consumers. Packaging which

74

incorporates features of augmented reality (i.e., graphic, audible or touch feedback elements) enhances the user experience, so explore the range of tech-savvy possibilities available to you. As it relates to your brand, consider having your package play music, release a scent or carry consumers into virtual reality territory. Or keep it simple. Always ask, "What makes sense for my brand?"

Whatever you do, use various aspects of your packaging to further build your brand image. In many instances, your package is the first touchpoint consumers have with your product. It should build your brand and prime customers for the grand experience of using what it is you have to offer. Don't stop at the feel and weight of your package. Consider how people will interact with it. Use language which evokes feeling and emotion to describe what's inside. Review every graphic element seen by consumers and people who'll be scanning your items to make sure it says something about your unique brand. View every element of your packaging as a part of the whole which works in tandem with the others to tell your brand story.

Bring them all together, in a way that tells the most delightful and compelling story possible.

Brand-Building Touchpoints:

- Build your brand image into your packaging experience.
- Let look, feel, texture and weight work in your favor.
- Ask whether your packaging delights consumers.
- Give voice to your brand via your packaging.

Your Brand Is Your Word Choice

What does your *word choice* say about your brand?

The language you use to describe and promote your brand plays a huge role in shaping how others perceive it. By being deliberate in your word choice, you get to tell people (through the thoughtful application of targeted language) what it is you're trying to build in conjunction with all of the other elements, which affect your branding efforts. Your color choices, your logo design, and your user experience—each of these subconsciously communicates something to your audience.

With brand language, though, you get to directly guide consumers to think what it is you *want* them to think, or believe, as it relates to your specific brand. Looking at it this way, it surprises me that so many business owners fail to consider the language they use across everything they do. How one restaurant owner speaks to potential diners about his Thai Fusion restaurant is usually quite similar to how another describes her Thai Fusion restaurant. Likewise, how one accountant describes her service offerings often deviates little from how a nearby competitor describes his.

When everyone uses the same language to describe what they produce, manufacture and ultimately sell, consumers are left thinking that each item being sold is more or less the same. So, what's the difference? They can go with you—or your competitor, right? (Please, no!) By not using your own language, or distinct brand voice, to guide audiences to think what it is you want them to think about the benefits your product or service offers, you leave your brand open to misinterpretation. You also leave a major brand-building opportunity on the table.

Speak Their Language

A great guide for customizing your word choice and developing related brand language for your business is to consider how members of your target audience speak to their peers. What language do they use to describe the types of products or services you're offering? How you speak about your own brand should be directly reflected in how they think about it, in their minds, or talk about it with friends and family. If your consumers have a rich vocabulary, brush up and expand your own. If you have a young and direct audience, use youthful language that quickly gets your point across.

You brand should sound as if it's part of the tribe your target market belongs to without trying too hard. You want your audience to be able to relate to you and to view your brand as *the* brand which understands them. But don't make it appear as if you're trying to fit in. Instead, just fit in! Even better? Become the leader of this tribe. Let them know that you're relatable, that you understand their needs and that you "get" what they're saying. For them to choose you, you must communicate that you know where they're coming from and where they want to go next.

So, how do you know what language to use? You listen. Listen to how these consumers speak to one another. Read reviews they've written about similar products, looking for clues about how they speak about brands like yours and the ideals (or values) they associate with the *idea* behind your brand. Your own target audience may include young, tech-savvy consumers. When they talk about eating at restaurants, though, their vocabulary may come from an emotional and primal place. These nuances are what you want to pick up on and build into your brand language.

How someone talks about one product or industry may not be how they speak about a completely different industry. Your goal is to find out how your audience speaks about what it is you want to create a dialogue around. You can uncover what people are saying in a few different ways. The first and most obvious way, though often overlooked, is to ask your target audience about what it is you offer them. Talk to your best customers and your worst customers, asking for insights. If you don't have any customers yet, talk to people you hope will be your customers.

When you do that, listen to the language they use. What are their frustrations? Where is their emphasis placed? Another important way to learn about the language your target audience uses is to get tuned in. Observe their conversations online, using social media to your advantage. Post questions to them on your social media pages. This is a great way to get feedback from large groups of people. Go to where they are online. Or just listen to what they say in public. These are all good ways to learn their language and to figure out how they like to interact.

Still, Choose Your Words Carefully

The slightest change in language can create a completely different brand image for you. Because of this, it's important that you choose and then use your language wisely on everything that comes in contact with your audience. That means website copy, packaging copy (as we discussed earlier), call scripts, email scripts and in-store signage. Review the examples below, which suggest different ways of welcoming people into your store or office. Try to imagine the different emotions, feelings and images each greeting creates:

- Yo!
- Welcome
- Well, come on in
- Hola! Pasen, por favor
- G'day, mate. Enjoy your stay!
- Greetings! Welcome to our store
- Greetings! Welcome to your new favorite store

They more or less say the same thing yet create very different images. How does your brand greet people?

Now, consider the impact of your choice of language across all of your brand communication tools: your website, your packaging, your marketing materials, your in-store displays and everywhere else language is used to form your brand image. This isn't confined to consumer-facing materials, either. Use the same diligence to arrive at the perfect language for use in your email signature, on internal documents and in shareholders' reports. I think you get the point. Everything that says anything about your business must have the right language on it, engineering communication so that it helps you create the brand you're hoping to build.

Keywords & Language Use Documents

Since your language will be used on everything your brand does, you may find it helpful to list out keywords your company must be sure to use—and *not* use. Include words and phrases, outlining when certain words or phrases should (and shouldn't) be applied. This tool isn't meant to slow down your team. Rather, it'll speed things up by keeping your brand integrity intact and making it so that teammates aren't searching for the perfect words every time. Imagine, for a moment, that one of your

Customer Service agents is trying to describe how a certain product should work. Wouldn't it be helpful for them to have a list of keywords describing how it works at their desk? While this may take the form of a call script, it could also be a simple list your agents can add their own personal flair to while still staying on-brand.

In addition, wouldn't you want every person who calls that department to be given the same, general explanation or product description? Think, too, about a time when you might be speaking to investors about your brand. Using consistent language, throughout your multiple conversations with that audience, will help them clearly envision what your brand is and why they should invest in it. By using the same language internally and externally, you solidify your brand message and your brand image. This also makes it easier for others to determine what it is you stand for.

Be bold about the words you use for your brand. If you worry about playing it safe too much of the time, you risk not creating an image at all. Your language should convey meaning, by evoking imagery and emotions that connect with people. If you need to use strong language to do this, by all means, use strong language. Don't worry about potentially offending or failing to connect with people outside of your target audience by way of your language choices. You don't want to connect with them anyway, since they're not your audience, and that's okay.

In today's day and age, your language may also include the use of emojis, abbreviations, acronyms or commonly-used slang. If you want to connect with a young, trendy female audience around a soul-feeding food brand that's crafted with care and made with love (aka products designed to help them show themselves a bit of love), the occasional use of a cupcake or pizza emoji may be warranted. Abbreviations like UR, IRL and OMG may also help you connect with consumers. Use them, if they make sense for your brand and if your consumer would be excited to know you use them. Just because you're a brand doesn't mean you can't or shouldn't use these forms of communication. Remember, you want to position your brand as being part of the larger tribe. If your target audience uses them, you'd be wise to use them, too!

Your word choice, or language, is the most obvious reflection of your brand. It tells your audience members that you're part of their tribe, that you get them and that you're relatable. Build your brand image through words, sentence structures, slang terms and abbreviations which make sense for you. Take time to study how your audience talks about the industry you're either in or entering, as this will help guide your language choices. Words are extremely powerful, so pull out a dictionary and a thesaurus. Find the perfect words to use for every situation and across every form of communication your brand puts out there.

Brand-Building Touchpoints:

- Be relatable, using the same language your consumers use.
- Use the same brand language consistently, building your brand along the way.
- Create a Keywords/Language Use document that influences all aspects of your business.

Your Brand Is How You Treat People

What does *how you treat people* say about your brand?

The products and services you offer comprise your brand. Yet, how you interact with consumers before, during and after a sale says a lot *about* your brand. Extra touches or special services shape your brand in the minds of consumers. These added touches can be small and simple, like delivering a mint along with the bill at a restaurant. They can be personal, like hand-delivering a product to someone's home. They can be practical, the way offering a lifelong guarantee on your product's durability would be. The opportunity—when engineering your brand this way—comes down to deciding how you want people to feel, in response to the little extras your business provides them with. Even the simplest acts can do wonders, in terms of any long-term success you have with building brand love and brand loyalty into the equation.

One of the biggest contributors to a great service experience with your brand is the people you hire, especially those who interact directly with your shoppers or consumers. To people who connect with them, these people *are* your brand. As such, they must be reflective of your brand. Let's imagine you run a professional, high-end clothing company. What it ultimately sells is the idea of looking, feeling and being well put together. You wouldn't want the staff in your stores to appear casual, rude or unkempt. This is not to say that you should discriminate in your hiring. Absolutely not. Simply hire people who are a right fit.

Those on the frontline of your brand need to embody it, so that your message comes through to consumers. When you're then selling that image, your sales team has an easier time of selling it for you, by representing that image themselves. This is true for a store with a physical presence where product is sold, a service company which has a receptionist on staff and a business-to-business firm that finds its staff connecting with suppliers, customers or business partners.

Set Service Guidelines

Anyone who serves as a representation of your brand needs to offer exceptional service that's on-target with your brand, so people walk away feeling great about the interaction and your brand itself. Think about the people who comprise your front line and who actually serve your customers: your in-store sales professionals, your receptionist, your B2B team. More often than not, they're the ones people think of when they picture your brand in their minds. Because they play such a critical role, it's best to create a set of policies or guidelines for how they interact with consumers.

Outline the entire service experience from start to finish on behalf of everyone you work with: from the very first interaction to the end of the very last transaction. If you own a store, should your staff stop what they're doing and come out from behind the counter to greet or shake your customer's hand? Should they walk consumers to the door after a purchase is made? Should they give out high fives with every purchase? Maybe you want them to wrap up by saying, "Have a killer day!" Or, "Have an awesome day!" Or, "Thank you for your business!".

Your choices should make sense for your business and should be a reflection of your brand. Obviously, those choices will differ. What remains the same, though, is your ability to control what your staff does to make sure that your brand walks out the door with your customers and that every customer enjoys the same, great experience of your brand—from beginning to end. Ask yourself, "What's our service experience like before someone even buys our product?"

Pre-sale service is another way to build your brand and, essentially, amounts to little things you can do to delight consumers before they even come through the doors. Online software-as-service companies do this extremely well with Free Trial offerings. Yes, this is obviously done to drive sales. But something as simple as this can help build your brand, by showing how helpful you can be and how committed you are to consumers' needs (even before they become paying customers).

Another pre-purchase strategy that works well is greeting people, as they enter your establishment, or greeting them in a particular way. Perhaps you offer them water, coffee or even a glass of wine. The right greeting for you will depend on your brand and what sort of relationships you're looking to build with you consumers. Just know that, when it comes to building your brand, little things absolutely matter. And that, when it comes to service, it's the details which differentiate.

Keep Surprising Them

How do people feel after they've purchased your product? Or, put another way, how can you continue to delight them after they've purchased from you? There are loads of opportunities to bring your brand to life here. Take advantage of them, deciding: how the sale should end, how a customer should be thanked and what you can send that customer after the sale. Maybe you'll choose to send consumers an e-newsletter that offers savings on their next purchase. Maybe they'll get a handwritten thank you note or a phone call to see how things are going with their purchase.

What you offer will vary based on industry and your choice of economy, mass or premium pricing tier. After all, the more someone invests in you (via your product or service) the more they expect from you. To show how you can build your brand after a sale has been made, let's walk through an example of how an online purchase with a coffee company could be used to build a brand. Let's assume this particular brand serves a masculine, direct and bold clientele. As soon as the order is placed a "Thank you for your order!" pop-up appears. Do you think that's enough to build this unique brand? What if, instead, the pop-up read: "John, you rock for ordering with us! We can't wait to fuel you up with a caffeine kick to the mouth—coming your way in the next 48 hours."

The second one makes you feel more connected to the brand, doesn't it? It helps develop the personality of the brand John is asking to connect with. "Thank you for your order!" demonstrates customer appreciation, but the latter option builds brand advocates. Let's take this a step further. Within this pop-up, perhaps there's a call to action. It asks John to share notification of his purchase on social media and contains a similar type of brand messaging or related image. With the simple click of a button, John can post to his network of friends how he's getting "a caffeine kick to the mouth" within 48 hours' time, when this brand of coffee arrives. Or he can share his basic, "Thank you …," message. Which one do you think has a better chance of being shared?

To continue to build brand advocacy through the checkout experience, John could be offered savings on his next order—after he shares news of his purchase with his friends. Or maybe he'll accumulate savings each time one of his friends uses his associated coupon code to place their own order with said coffee brand. John now has multiple ways to be committed to something that could otherwise be quite functional: coffee. All of this brand building is happening within the space of a simple thank you process.

Then there's the email John gets after the purchase, confirming shipping details and the fact that his order went through. Shouldn't this be used to bring the brand to life, too? Don't just tell John that his order is confirmed. Tell him when his order will arrive, so he can begin to anticipate that "caffeine kick to the mouth" he's looking forward to. Taking it another step further, it could include a cheeky line about hoping he can stay awake until his order arrives and that, if not, you hope his boss will understand.

Next up is the delivery itself. Make sure that your own delivery schedule is in line with what your brand promises. If your brand is all about handcrafted goodness, chances are consumers will be patient and expect a longer delivery time. If, however, you're providing your consumer with items which are needed immediately (or your brand operates on an "efficiency" brand platform), you'd better make sure that what you're selling is delivered on time and as quickly as possible.

Once the product is delivered, what does this look like? Is it packaged in a well-branded, high-quality, corrugated shipping box? Does it have a bow on it, a branded sticker or arrive in a uniquely-colored shipping bag? Was it delivered by standard mail, express mail or your company mascot? All of these details add up to a means for engineering your brand so that it conveys strong, positive associations before someone has even gotten to the product itself.

Enhance Your Memorability

If you own a restaurant or retail store, there are lots of ways to bring post-sale service to life. What does your receipt say? Chances are it says, basically, the same thing as everyone else's receipt within your industry and outside of your industry. Use it as an opportunity to enhance your memorability even more, adding a line or two to strengthen your brand. Share unique facts about your product, your business or your industry. Make it something of interest and change it up now and then, so guests begin to look forward to seeing what you'll share next. Tips which help consumers use your products or build the lifestyle your brand stands for are other great ideas.

If what you offer is portable, what type of bag do customers receive to carry the product home in? Do its materials, language (aka copy) and shape build your brand in some way? The same principles which apply to building your brand through packaging should be applied to any bag or box consumers use to carry their purchases proudly out of your store. How their purchase items are placed within that bag or box is also something you can control, engineering your brand message even more. Think of additional items you can include with the item being sold: flyers, postcards, stickers, etc. The fact that an item is folded in colored tissue paper, folded without tissue paper or wrapped in recycled newspaper builds a different, lasting image of your brand.

If you're a service provider or product manufacturer, do you offer 24-hour or other forms of customer service? Bundle that information into your packaging. Throw in a few coupons the consumer can share with friends. Offer incentives which make customers want to buy from you again and again. Include a complimentary product with their purchase; one that will, of course, help build your brand. If you sell lipstick, can a small mirror be included—one that features your logo? If you're selling a suit, a coupon for a trusted dry cleaner would likely be a big hit. Find ways to delight customers after they purchase from you and your chances of having them become repeat customers will increase!

Little Things Add Up

Small acts of kindness add up. So do each of the little things you add to your product or service mix, as a way of expressing genuine interest in your customer relationships. We discussed building your brand after the sale by including an edible treat or by making sure someone makes a follow-up call. Those will build your brand and make you more memorable for sure. Yet, any opportunity you take to connect with the people who comprise your customer base is a sure way to help them form a higher opinion of your brand, overall, and to stand out from the competition.

Even if someone isn't 100% satisfied with the product or service you've sold them (we'll talk about that below), offering strong after-sale service will make them more forgiving of anything they didn't particularly like about the transaction. The fact that you even address their concerns, in a phone call or online, will prove that you do care. And I know you do care. This is a great time to think about your exchange and warranty policies, as well. They must also be evaluated to be sure they sync up with your other efforts at building your brand.

It could be that you don't offer a warranty at all, given the nature of your particular product or service. Or that you offer a small window of time in which consumers can contact you to make the situation right. If your own brand is all about quality and responsibility, it makes sense to have a strong return or warranty policy. Patagonia®, an outdoor lifestyle and active clothing brand, does a fantastic job of bringing quality to life with its lifetime return policy. That's right—lifetime! The brand stands proudly behind the quality of its items, which is apparent in: the materials it uses, the multifunctional nature of its items and the overall delivery of its products.

For Patagonia, quality means its products should be able to accompany you on all of the adventures you set out to experience and then stand the test of time. Whether climbing mountains, hiking in the outback, canoeing, camping or anything in between, its products should last and last. In response, it allows the return of any item. That's true whether it's ripped, torn or simply didn't perform the way you expected it to. If you don't want to return it, since you love it so much (flaws and all) or because it's been discontinued, no problem. Patagonia will fix it for free.

The message conveyed by this strong warranty program is that Patagonia stands firmly behind the quality and durability of its product line. As a result, it's easy to trust the brand. When we think of quality, we can think positively about what it is the brand says and then does to back up its claims. It's not hard to believe that the people behind the brand make products of the highest quality, given their terms. While this may not make sense for your brand or may seem extreme, I'm sure there's a way you can design a program of extra little touches that will wow your own customers.

Take Control of Potential Complaints

How you handle complaints says a lot about your brand, as well. No matter how great your product or service is, you're bound to receive less than stellar feedback from time to time. The way you and your staff receive and react to it determines whether you're able to calm an upset customer or wind up turning an unhappy customer into one who's fuming mad. The best time to think about how you'll handle such complaints is now. So, don't wait: Put sensible return, warranty and customer management practices into place immediately.

Alone and with your staff, if you have any, consider all of the potential issues which could arise regarding your product or service. Then, list out ways you can best resolve those issues. Your solutions should help you remain on-brand and preserve your brand image. Include, in your list:

- All foreseeable issues/concerns
- Actions you will take for each one
- Who'll be responsible for following up
- Turnaround time: immediate, 24-hour, etc.
- Technologies to be used (i.e., phone, email)
- The best brand language to address each issue

Think about what else you can do that's on-brand to mitigate an issue. If you're a software vendor, you might upgrade a disgruntled customer's product at no extra cost. If you own a café, you might give the customer a free mug, tote or muffin. It also helps to be clear about who within your organization is able to authorize returns, discounts and free merchandise— with the goal of quickly and easily turning a bad brand experience into a good one. The more you empower your employees, the less likely it is the problem will escalate or get out of hand. Still, maintain control over the process. A sure way to do that is by making problem resolution a priority here and now.

Your brand is affected by your products, services and ability to manage the experience you give consumers. The way you treat them leaves an impression of your brand that will last long after you've completed a transaction together. Everything you do before they buy until after they make a purchase works in tandem to reinforce your brand message and to forge positive connections with your brand image. Take every opportunity you're given and build it into a strong experience. Whether that includes free samples upfront or a simple return process, be sure people are treated to a great brand experience in-store, online and over the phone.

A frontline staff that embodies your brand strengthens those efforts. Treat them right, too!

Brand-Building Touchpoints:

- Do little things to improve consumers' experiences with you.
- Task your frontline staff with bringing your brand to life.
- Make each interaction with your customers count.
- Empower your staff to solve problems quickly.

Your Brand Is Your Experience

What does your *experience* say about your brand?

There are two ways you can approach doing business as a brand. You can either offer consumers a unique experience or you can make every encounter with your brand a mere transactional one. I'm in favor of unique experiences. How about you? It may very well be the case that most of your day-to-day interactions are transaction-based. However, if you turn those interactions into bona fide experiences, you'll do more to solidify your brand and to get others excited about it. So, whenever possible, provide consumers with unusual or extraordinary experiences they can't get elsewhere.

The experience you create can be as grand and all-encompassing as what Disney® has done through its theme parks, merchandise and movie franchise. Or it be as simple as an intimate, invite-only gathering of your best customers to help celebrate a product launch, business anniversary or other special event. The experience of a retail store alone can even be enough, when you consider what Apple has created. In total, the experiences you create build upon your brand and are reflective of your brand—in the eyes of consumers.

It's likely that a typical consumer has brief and infrequent interactions with your brand. Yet, using your website, mobile app and social media accounts as platforms for regularly interacting with them can also result in new experiences for them. No matter what you do to create some buzz and excitement around your brand, engineer those activities so that you create the kind of experience consumers expect or want from you and your brand.

Design a Powerful User Experience

User Experience, otherwise known as UX refers to anything design-related that's meant to enhance how a given consumer experiences your brand. This can be as simple as how someone moves through your business app and what that tells them about your brand. Things to pay attention to are: how the app opens, which sorts of icons people click on to get additional content, how content renders on mobile devices or desktop computers and how intuitive the swiping is, left, right, up and down.

UX design isn't just applicable to developing tech products. It applies to every possible way a consumer can experience any type of product. How something will be opened, where a zipper is placed, what materials are used to reseal a bag—each of these encounters helps build the image of your brand. All of them are to be considered, when you're designing (and, therefore, engineering) the entire experience that comes with using and enjoying your product or service.

Still, I want to help you expand your brand experience in a number of ways. Think of it in relationship to the day-to-day connection points you share with your consumers and as a way of interacting with consumers beyond the day-to-day. The goal is to make each type of experience extremely impactful, crafting a brand that's not soon forgotten and communicating the ideas and purpose behind it. Let's look at the most extreme version of creating a brand experience I can think of: Disneyland®. Disney created an entire theme park around its brand, resulting in the ultimate branded experience for adoring kids and adults in the U.S. and across the globe.

Truly Engineer Your Experience

Patrons are eagerly welcomed to "the happiest place on earth" upon arriving at Disneyland. Every aspect of their visit, in fact, is designed to make it feel like the happiest place on earth. At the same time, it helps build a deep-rooted love for the Disney brand through meaningful play. Whether getting a photo taken with a favorite character, going on a ride that plunges you into the world of a beloved film or buying a pair of Mickey Mouse® ears your kid will continue to wear every day for the next three months, everything about the theme park is engineered to create a magical and unforgettable experience which turns Disney customers into Disney advocates.

People's connections with Disneyland and the Disney brand run deep, as a result. While most brands don't have a budget that would allow them to open up theme parks, in hopes of creating the ultimate brand experience, most can lead or sponsor seasonal or other events aimed at building their brands. These events—like everything else you do for your brand—should be done with the goal of connecting with your audience, as well as putting the experiences and emotions you want people to associate with it on steroids. If you want people to connect excitement with your brand, you might sponsor a whitewater rafting adventure. If you want them to feel refreshed, sponsor or set up cooling stations near your store in summertime. Think about what you want consumers to feel, when they think of your brand, and engineer that same feeling into an experience you can easily offer them.

I once ran an event that revolved around a new premium line of Campbell's Soup. The goal was to get consumers to view the soup we were selling as fresh-tasting and as good as (if not better than) homemade. How did we bring this freshness and a sense of homemade-ness to life? We created a sampling booth and lined its entire back wall with fresh herbs. This living wall was the backdrop against which the soup was served. Fresh basil, parsley and oregano created bright, familiar scents. As people walked by, they were intrigued and eager to taste the product. That was due to the fresh scents they now associated with it. People were served flute glasses full of these deliciously thick soups—with fresh herbs set on top, just like how someone might garnish them at home. By setting an accurate premium, fresh and out-of-the-ordinary tone for this experience, we were able to position the brand as a premium soup product in consumers' minds.

Host Your Own Event

Your own event should evoke the same emotions in your audience that you want your brand to evoke in your audience. It should also embody your brand and build a connection to it. If you're in the wine business, consider a wine and cheese tasting event. But don't stop there! Think of all the different ways you can make the experience more authentic or vivid for your guests. Host it at a winery versus in-store. Hold it at a restaurant nearby and offer a shuttle service from your store. Give away "Wine & Cheese Pairing" tip sheets or even fresh cheese to event participants.

Partner with a foundation that maintains a historic homestead and schedule your wine and cheese tasting there. If desired, advertise and then ensure that a portion of event ticket pricing is donated to the foundation, as a way of contributing to upkeep of the local treasure. Each variation on the same event can create and highlight a completely different persona or aspect of your brand. Decide what it is you want your audience and event participants to walk away feeling. Make every decision about your event based against this checkpoint.

If you want people to think of your wine and cheese event as being authentic, then maybe the winery would make sense. If, instead, you're trying to get people to think of your brand as being the perfect pairing for lively casual functions, then holding it in the restaurant makes more sense. If you're going for a relaxed and homey feel, then book the historic landmark. Your choice of venue and resulting event will differ for different audiences, but should always reflect your brand and seek to draw in people who comprise your most ideal target market or audience.

When hosting any event, an array of details can either help or hurt your brand. A few areas of event planning you should consider, in advance, follow. This list is just a sampling:

- *Food/Drink* – catered, open bar, cash bar, no bar
- *Venue* – location, décor, accessibility, music options
- *Wait staff* – appearance, mannerisms, service offerings
- *Timing* – day of the week, time of day, duration, event schedule
- *Guest list* – existing customers, staff, community leaders, partners
- *Other* – swag bags, complimentary samples, cross-vendor promotions

Every detail should be planned out, when building your brand experience. Even if you're planning an experience that's as seemingly simple as handing out samples on the street, ask yourself: What street best connects with my brand? What time of day will my brand resonate most with passersby? What should sampling staff wear to build the brand further? What should they say and hand out to people? Building branded experiences really comes down to the tiniest of details.

Craft Your Retail Experience

Creating an experience for your retail location is an important element in exceptional brand building. If you haven't yet built your store experience in a way that's unique, how will people know they've entered your store and not a competitor's? If people can't distinguish you from your competition by something other than a sign on the front of the building, you already have a great opportunity to enhance their experience.

Store layout also impacts the consumer experience. Are products displayed across every square inch of your store, leaving a feeling of abundance with shoppers? Are items grouped sparsely, creating an airy and open feel? Or is so little product on display that customers feel they are getting one of a kind from you? Are there digital screens throughout your store? When people enter your store, what happens? When they're in a changing room are they completely forgotten about? Are there ample mirrors and lighting? What do their interactions with staff look like? Do scent, music and lighting serve to enhance or detract from your customer experience and brand image?

When it gets to the point where people can "feel" your brand, as they step into your store, you've made it easy for them to connect with your product. You've created a connection point with them before they've purchased a thing. If they're the right consumer, they'll value the brand experience you've provided and feel as if it's perfectly designed with them in mind.

Think about the Apple store again, this time from an experiential standpoint. Apple has created a store experience that literally draws in youth who come to hang out and check on what's new. Apple knows lots of people love its products, in part due to the user experience it's designed around those products. It builds simplicity, sleek design and efficiency into its store locations. Its products are similarly easy-to-use, sleek and cutting edge—contributing to consumer efficiency and productivity. Tech types love to touch and play around with them.

Knowing this, Apple has designed its store experience accordingly. It's as if the company is saying, "Come on in and play around with the newest technology. Experience its benefits for yourself. Touch a few buttons. You won't hurt anything!"

Apple staff contributes to building the store experience, too. They don't stand back and wait for people to come to them. Nope. They roam the floors and mingle with guests, dressed in whatever colored shirt the team is wearing that season. They ask if people have questions, showing them how to use the latest products and even checking people out on-the-spot using handheld devices. This is an extremely different experience than you'll get in most any other retail store today.

Consider Your Own Business

What kind of experience can you create for your shoppers? If you're a service provider, how can you include customers in what you do? If you own an outdoor adventure store, do you have tents set up? Is the scent of s'mores, pinecones or campfires circulating through the air? Are the floorboards bright and shiny or do they look rustic? Do the images on your walls inspire adventure in your shoppers? If yours is a sporting goods store, I'd hope you at least have one TV running which is set to a popular sports channel. Heck, maybe you've replicated a stadium food stand and sell game day fare or throw in-store tailgate parties!

Sticking with in-store experiences, what about store design? Is there a way to create a tie-in with your brand? If you run a sporting goods store, can your floors be painted or tiled to resemble a playing field? If you own an art supply store or gallery space, are there walls people can paint or draw directly on? If you have a clothing store, it's always best to have more mirrors than you can handle—so people can quickly see how great they look in your clothes.

The key, whether you're a product or service provider, is to tap into the minds of your shoppers and imagine what will "Wow!" them most. At a bare minimum, be sure everyone has a pleasant experience and isn't left wanting. Decide what they expect from you and do that, plus a bit extra. Make doing business with you easy, putting technology in place whenever possible. Make your physical or online space easy to navigate. Make sure you're the best part of your customers' day, building your brand and their love for your brand at the same time.

Use strong brand experiences, too, to fast track your connection with consumers. This is done by tapping into emotions and values which matter to both of you. It's done through deliberate UX design of products and services. It's done by hosting events which help them make sense of what it is you do and what you have to offer them. It's done, more overtly, by creating holistic branded experiences like those encountered at Disneyland. It's done, in retail, by evoking a sense that your store is where they belong. All of it results in them wanting to spend more time with *your* brand.

Brand-Building Touchpoints:

- Consciously engineer every step of your brand experience.
- Do that in-store, online and, especially, through events.
- Aim to make people feel connected with your brand, by delivering experiences which delight them.

Your Brand Is Your Culture

What does your *culture* say about your brand?

Famed businessman Peter Drucker coined the term "culture eats strategy for breakfast" and it's since influenced the way thousands of companies run their businesses. Many people like to think that strategy without execution means nothing. Yet, when you view business through Drucker's eyes, you see that you can't get strategy or execution right if you don't have the right culture in place. Your brand is your culture, because it's through the people you hire and the environment you create that your brand comes to life and connects with others.

Today's employees are more inclined to work for companies aligned with their own beliefs and work styles than simply companies which pay well. Telling them who you are and why they should want to join your team is part of how you grow your culture and, ultimately, your brand. The right culture is a crucial element in building your brand. When done well, it can take your business to the next level and become something people think of when they think of your brand.

What Is Culture, Anyway?

When consumers think of Google®, they think of the search engine platform, yes. But the company has also become synonymous with having a culture like none other. Its employees are treated to free, delicious and healthy meals all day long. Its brainstorm rooms are decked out with hammocks and tents. It has its own sports teams, offers music lessons on-site and allows people to spend company time working on projects and assignments which aren't directly connected to their actual job titles but allow them to explore their passions. The list of perks goes on. It's no wonder holding a position at Google seems like a dream job for many people or that Google ranked No. 3 on *Forbes* magazine's 2018 list of "Top 25 Companies" to work for, in America, based on culture and values.

Salesforce®, a leading cloud-based company offering customer relationship management (CRM) services, is also revered as a great place to work. It received top honors, in 2017, when it ranked No. 1 on *Forbes* magazine's list of "Most Innovative Companies" in the U.S. Its cultural guidepost is the Hawaiian ideology of Ohana, which symbolizes togetherness, cooperation and consideration; the idea that each person should be treated equally and should also be treated like family. Salesforce applies the Ohana method with everyone connected to its brand. Employees, partners and customers are all treated as equals who are dealt with fairly. The company lives and breathes this idea, first applying the Ohana method with its employees. In turn, this encourages employees to use the same mindset when interacting with customers, colleagues and other business partners. In this way, its positive culture grows.

How everything is done, within Salesforce, is informed by the Ohana method. Products are designed with the "family" concept in mind. Negotiations occur between "family" members rather than between "the company" and its "clients." Everyday conversations and decisions unfold in fair and transparent ways, to ensure that there is no bad blood running between them. Rather, the focus is on making the entire team/family unit stronger. This culture affects what happens on the phone, in the boardroom and, as a result, in consumers' minds.

Google and Salesforce are both onto something here. Gallup noted, in its 2017 "State of the American Workplace" study, that employees who are engaged with their work are more likely to improve their customer relationships, resulting in a 20% increase of sales. Happy employees lead to happy customers—and happy bottom lines. If you want to succeed, to stand out and to have everyone live and breathe your brand from the inside out, it's extremely important to build a culture people want to engage with and to make sure that your culture embodies your brand. Common elements of a great culture include:

- Trust
- Teamwork
- Recognition
- Transparency
- Communication

What these elements of culture mean for your company is up to you. One business leader may choose to implement recognition by buying coffee, or lunch, for an employee who's done a great job of serving a particular customer. Another may decide that recognition is best delivered in the form of a handwritten note. Yet another may decide that recognition warrants acknowledgement in front of the entire company. Find ways to put creative twists on these, making them your own.

Hire with Culture in Mind

The values your brand embodies need to live in your employees. Because your employees are your brand, hire people who stand for what your brand represents. These are the people who will live your brand and fight for it. If you don't have people who are willing to fight for your brand, chances are you won't have a brand that lasts very long. Hiring employees who embody the same values as your brand makes it easy for them to know how to operate and how to pass on the vision of that brand to customers through the work they do.

Now, I'm not saying you should hire from within your target market and only your target market. In fact, I urge you not to. If you do, you risk having a close-minded organization and finding yourself trapped in a bubble that limits your growth and thought process. Instead, when you hire for your brand, hire based on the qualities your brand stands for. Say, for example, you make and sell a plant-based protein powder targeted to marathon athletes for whom supplementation is part of their overall path to wellness. While you very well might end up hiring people who are marathon runners and follow plant-based diets, your brand's core belief is likely about "bettering oneself." Hiring an avid scrapbooker may still make sense, if they use that activity to better themselves.

Take, for instance, my own company. At Engineer Your Brand, we value and stand for building remarkable brand connections between business owners and their target audiences. With this, I personally ensure that every person who comes on board is genuinely interested in creating remarkable experiences for the people we serve. This is different from merely doing the task at hand or a delivering a job on time. While both of these are absolutely necessary and are part of our culture, one of the core qualities I look for in employees is a willingness to go above and beyond to truly create remarkable experiences for our clients. One thing I always ask a potential new hire is what they believe their life purpose is. This can be a daunting question, I know. While the answer is important, it's equally important to get an understanding of whether the person has taken any time—up until now—to think about this.

When you're hiring, consider the characteristics you want your brand to embody and then look for those traits in potential candidates. Take the time to find people who are a right fit for you and the culture you're looking to build. If you have a brand that's lighthearted and playful, be sure to assess candidates for these qualities during your interview process. Maybe you ask an overt question like, "What's the silliest thing you've done this week?" If you don't want to be so overt, observe to see whether candidates insert an element of humor in their answers to your questions.

By selecting people who are excited about what you do, you can pretty much guarantee they'll do it with enthusiasm. They'll do it passionately. They'll do it in ways which make sense for your brand. Your employees become the advocates for your brand. Done right, hiring can be extremely powerful for your brand—especially as you grow and certainly during any tough times your business may encounter.

Culture & Employee Pride

I felt the power of getting your employees fully behind your brand when I worked for Coca-Cola. Every person I met, who also worked at Coca-Cola, loved working for the brand. That doesn't mean they all necessarily loved the products themselves, although many do. It does mean they love the brand itself. Employees buy into any new launches which are happening and get genuinely excited that consumers will soon have access to these new products once they hit the market. They buy into the process, wanting to create elaborate in-store displays built entirely out of cases of Coca-Cola. They're excited by the company's history and growth. They feel a sense of pride working for this brand. As a result, they bring a true sense of excitement to their work and always have a winning attitude when it comes to outperforming "the blue guys" (aka Pepsi®).

I remember that my loyalty to the brand was so strong that I wouldn't even allow my friends or family to serve Pepsi products when I was around. The Coca-Cola culture of winning against "the blue guys" with every soda occasion had ingrained in me an absolute desire to never drink or support a challenger's product. The market was just too competitive. Anyway, in our collective view, the other guys weren't as good anyway. We couldn't allow people to support them, if we had a say in it. Coca-Cola employees have such a strong desire to win that team events and casual lunches would never be held in locations which served competing brands. If we somehow ended up at a location that didn't serve Coca-Cola products, tap water was the only thing we would drink.

This level of internal brand love should be a goal of your own company's culture. You can achieve that by asking yourself a few simple questions:

- How can I make my culture so strong that my employees live and breathe it, both during work hours and after work hours?
- How can I get them so passionate about the brand and so ingrained in its culture that they feel a sense of pride, experience a deep-rooted affiliation and are truly vested in its success?

I'm a believer that it's easier to teach a skill than it is to teach culture. Obviously, new employees need to be brought up to speed on what the culture within the business is really like. Yet, I exercise caution and err on the side of making sure no one I bring on board is too far off from the culture I'm looking to create. It only takes a few people who are out of sync with company culture to throw it entirely out of whack and erode everything you've worked so hard to create. So, when it comes to selecting the right people to represent your brand, hire slow and fire fast.

Let Your Office Do the Talking

Your office is also a reflection of your culture and your brand. Set yours up so that staff, vendors and customers quickly get a sense for your brand at every turn. This step is crucially important in showcasing your brand and reinforcing the type of culture you're creating around it.

First and foremost, consider where your office will be located. If your brand is built for social and outgoing trendsetters, it won't make sense for your office to be situated in the suburbs—no matter how much cheaper the rent is. You need to be where it makes sense for your brand to be. In this case, that's likely in a not-so-cheap downtown location. Imagine your brand being a person. Would your brand live out in the suburbs near an elementary school? Or in the city near the best shops, bars and restaurants?

After you've got an office space selected, the décor and layout can be thought through. Again, it's helpful to think about your brand as if it were a person here. What art would this individual hang on the walls? What would their rooms look like? What would their kitchen space look like? Would their living area be a flowing open-concept or would it be walled off and sterile? What extra touches would occupy the room, if your brand was actually a person?

Unilever® (the parent company to Axe®, Dove®, Knorr®, Vaseline® and other multimillion-dollar household brands) does this phenomenally. Being a company of this size, its office space has numerous boardrooms. Every boardroom needs a name, so that people know where they're going. The company took this opportunity to name each room after one if its brands. Not only that but each room is decorated as if it's a room that would be used by a member of its target audience. The Knorr room is filled with imagery of fresh food, fresh ingredients, chefs and families enjoying meals together. It's quite different from the Axe body spray room, which is set up to feel as if it's the dream suite of one of the teenage boys you'd see advertising the product in commercials.

Unilever has done this for the largest and most prominent brands it owns. When a meeting is held about a particular brand you would, of course, head to its respective room—so you can get into the mindset of that consumer and that brand. This is why décor is important to office design. It's a way to connect your employees to your brand and to give target audience members every opportunity to experience what your brand embodies and how it can be thought about in real-world scenarios rather than through abstract ideas involving hypothetical people. Maybe you only have one target audience. Great! Set up a space in your office that embodies this person, so they'll always be top of mind.

This pertains to other elements of office design, as well. Do you need couches for people to brainstorm on? Do you need a gym to help promote healthy living and an active mind? Do you need a barista or juicer on staff? These things may seem like nice-to-haves, but they really aren't. They're there to build culture, which then gets the best out of your team and allows it, in turn, to help build your brand for you.

You should also ask yourself whether an office is necessary at all. More and more companies today are opting for flexible workspaces or no workspaces at all. Maybe there is an office, but no one has assigned seating and there certainly isn't enough seating for everyone to be in the office at the same time anyway. Or, maybe, everyone works from home all the time or people work out of shared office spaces alongside other businesses. It's easier to build culture from having central office locations, but you can certainly build culture from remote workspaces or shared workspaces too.

Ask yourself what your brand needs and what would make your team truly able to deliver on your brand promise. Even if you're using shared office space, it should reflect your brand the same way selecting a home office would. Is the shared office warm and friendly—or is it cold and unapproachable? Is it open 24 hours or only during core business hours? Is it downtown or uptown? It's still important to embody your brand, though with shared office spaces you just won't have as much control over the variables. Remember that wherever your space is it will influence you and it will influence what other people think about your brand, when they visit you on-site or when they hear about the office space you're working from.

Give Your Team Structure

Your brand will live within your employees, so it's important to set up a team structure which reflects the brand you're creating. This includes researching and implementing the right management style, as well as determining how your teams will operate and work with one another. Do you want a team of people working together to find solutions to day-to-day or unique problems? Or do you want someone more experienced at the top, guiding the way your business and its teams solve problems? Your answer to this should be reflected in how management operates with everyone and how your employees work with one another. Whether or not management sits in their corner offices or amongst their teams does change the brand you're building. Same goes if you have all members of a given division sit only with one another or integrate with people who are performing various other functions.

Team structure and management style comprise a fundamental element of your brand. With this, I encourage you not to put this off to some point in the future—such as when your brand reaches a certain revenue target or you hire a set number of employees. Building and changing culture is not easy, so taking the time to craft it from as early on as possible can help give it a solid foundation. If you don't intentionally build your culture, chances are it will evolve into something on its own. That something may be exactly what you want for your brand. More likely, though, it won't. Take the time to engineer your culture the same way you do every other element of your brand.

What titles can you use to bring your brand to life and showcase to others what it is your people really do? Employee titles are reflective of your brand both internally and externally. Everyone wants to know who someone is and what their role is at a company. This curiosity comes from internal employees as well as from outside vendors. Don't overlook the opportunity to position your brand and your people through the use of titles. If the goal of a title is to tell people what someone does, then really tell people what it is they do and build your brand while you're at it.

There's a big difference between someone's title being Executive Assistant, Right Hand of the President, Office Sheep Herder or Office Coordinator. All of these bring different visions to mind—not only about the person behind the title but also about what they do and the type of company they do it for.

Culture & Related Behaviors

How your people behave is also a reflection of your brand. What are the ways of being within your company? These can be viewed as policies for your brand. Basically, though, they're a set of standards for how the people

114

who represent your brand will act. You can set standards regarding wardrobe, work hours, response times, hiring terms, remote working and many other policy items. The key is to have them promote the development of your culture and your brand, since these are the little things which reflect and build your brand on an ongoing basis.

Think about how different it would be to brainstorm with a roomful of people who are wearing ripped jeans and T-shirts versus business suits and ties. I'm going to say that the creativity and output levels of these two groups—even if they were made up of the exact same people—would differ solely based on the level of creativity that was fostered through wardrobe standards. Similarly, what might your office hours say about your brand culture? Do you want people to be in the office from 9 a.m. to 5 p.m. every weekday? Should they come in for a few hours each day? Or, if what you have is a remote work team, not at all? Think about what's needed for your brand to thrive and for you to create a culture that brings it to life. Be intentional about engineering your hours and other ways of being.

Stay Connected

Stay connected in ways which help everyone build your brand vision. Decide how your employees will communicate with one another and with clients. Are people trained to walk to one another's desks or are they writing emails to one another? Are they phoning or texting or communicating on another platform like Slack® or Telegram®? The right way to communicate with one another and with clients is part of your culture, so put some real thought into it.

Whatever platforms you use, everyone should be trained on them and should be encouraged to use them (as much as possible) to maintain the consistency and culture you're going after. The idea is to use the communication technology which makes the most sense for your brand. If your brand is a highly engaged and social brand, maybe you all connect to one another via Snapchat® or video messaging anytime you can't work side-by-side. On the other hand, if you have a highly technical product, emails and phone calls may be best so that people can reference important and detailed information relevant to your conversations.

Also think about how you communicate externally. Do you call clients? Do you have chatbots communicate with your customers? What's in your email signature and outgoing voicemail message? All of these elements need to be thought of in terms of your brand. How can you make your brand known through each of these interactions? At one point I owned a coffee company which served people who only drank their coffee black. Each email signature stated how long the person had been a black coffee drinker. In a similar vein, I worked with a company that had won plenty of awards in the past. We made sure that all company signatures on email signoffs listed the awards the company had won.

Transform little things like email, voicemail, sticky notes and boardroom names into ways you can build your brand for everyone they come in contact with. View each of these as an opportunity to promote a culture, which contributes to your brand building. For them to do the same, people within and outside of your business need to see that you live and breathe the brand itself. If you expect your brand to be wild and exciting, create that sort of environment and culture for your employees. Otherwise, there's no way they will strive to or can be expected to create the same experience for your customers.

Brand-Building Touchpoints:

- Hire based on culture more than skillset.
- Set up your workspace so it's reflective of your brand.
- Help others get in the mindset of your brand often and easily.
- Use operating standards as another way to build brand culture.

Your Brand Is Your Font

What does your *font* say about your brand?

The font, or typeface, you use and how you use it can change the meaning of your words and the ideas evoked by your brand. Finding the right font for your brand will help you connect with your audience, build your unique image and, of course, help people read your messages more clearly. This will make you more effective at telling them all about your brand. In addition to selecting the right font, how you treat it also impacts the meaning you convey. Things like font spacing, boldness and appearance together help further engineer the brand you're looking to create.

Let's start by defining two different terms related to lettering. The first is *font*, which is the actual typeface you use. The most popular fonts are Arial, Times New Roman and Calibri. The second term is *typography*. Typography is the overarching family name under which the full range of fonts are categorized. There are four main typographies, each capable of communicating different aspects of your brand. Once you've selected the typography category that best represents your brand, you can select the best font to represent your brand. The four typography groupings are outlined in this chapter along with examples of fonts which fall under each one. More importantly, I've laid out what each typography grouping is likely to communicate to your audience.

Serif Fonts

Serif fonts are the most traditional styles of all. They can be distinguished by the little sticks or feet which appear within each letter. Serif fonts should be used when trying to communicate trust (those little sticks/feet suggest stability) and establish a level of familiarity with your brand, both of which their look conveys. Serif fonts represent feelings of comfort, familiarity, tradition, reliability, sophistication, pragmatism and formality. Examples include:

- Garamond
- Times New Roman
- Courier
- Palatino

Sans Serif Fonts

Then there are Sans Serif fonts, which are more universal. These fonts are noticeably missing the little sticks or feet which appear in Serif fonts. They are best suited to modern, new and forward-looking brands. Thanks to their clean lines, Sans Serif fonts represent modernity, objectivity, newness, freshness, sleekness and clarity. Examples include:

- Helvetica
- Arial
- Geneva
- Calibri

Script Fonts

Script fonts are more elegant in nature and work well with luxury brands. These literally look as if someone took the time to write them out by hand.

They're more formal, sophisticated, elegant and stylish than both Serif and Sans Serif font types. Examples include:

- *Snell Roundhand*
- *Apple Chancery*
- ***Brush Script***
- *Edwardian Script*

Display Fonts

Display fonts are decorative, making them friendlier. Though, depending on your selection, they can appear more juvenile. Choose a Display font to communicate amusement, to be expressive or to show that your brand is unique, playful and youthful. These work especially well when you want your brand to appeal to a small, specific niche. Examples include:

- Rockwell
- **Impact**
- **STENCIL**
- **ROSEWOOD**

Each of your font choices should be selected intentionally, so that you bring emotions to life and build the sorts of connections you want people to have with your brand. As you can see from the image included here, there are a variety of ways to use fonts to convey a range of emotions and ideas associated with a brand. Different brands use different fonts selectively and consistently; building images of themselves we know and love today. How many of them do you recognize?

When selecting your fonts, I recommend choosing three different fonts which will work well together: your main font, your heading font and your accent font. Your main font is just that. It's the one which will most often be associated with your brand. This may or may not be the font you use in your logo. Your heading font will be used in conjunction with your main font, as a way of complementing it and emphasizing various aspects of your copy. It will be used in the headline on different elements of your packaging, website and everything else—so, it should be bolder than your main font choice. Its treatment will either be bold or script, drawing extra attention to itself.

Any accent font you select will be used far less often and should capture people's attention. Use it on an infrequent basis, such as when you want to make a bold statement stand out. It can serve as a heading on a webpage that calls out a sale, a limited-time offer, a special offer, etc. Accent fonts are usually the boldest of all of your three font choices. These are the ones which grab people's attention the most.

Font Treatments

Highlighting text by using bold or italics draws attention to it. Used only as needed, these are great ways to emphasize certain messages or aspects of your brand. Don't go overboard, by having everything written in bold or italic type or by using special punctuation everywhere. Like anything, moderation is key. Bold type communicates that a statement is dominant, strong and significant. Use it to create this effect. Italics, on the other hand, provide a sense of motion or movement. Both are intended to make your words appear distinct, driving emphasis—and eyes—to them.

The spacing between your letters also has an impact on your brand. If you want to create a tight-knit, put-together and buttoned-up brand, you may want your typeface letters to be more closely aligned with one another. Whereas, if you're aiming to create an airy and carefree brand, look for ways to add a bit more spacing between the letters. This subtle difference can have a massive impact on how people read and, in turn, feel about the information you're sharing and the brand you're building.

The power of your brand really comes to life through font choice by registering with readers on a subconscious level. This subconscious reach is such an important element of branding, because it works behind the scenes to have people think what it is you want them to think when they think of you. The more influencing you can do below the surface to create the image you want for your brand, the more it will resonate with the right consumers. Ultimately, this will lead to them trusting you, connecting with you and wanting to build relationships with you. Most notably, it will drive them to want to buy your specific product or service.

Your font shapes your brand through how it reads and through the messages it imprints in readers' minds. Everything from the selection itself to when and how you use bold or italic type and how you set your spacing helps guide readers to better understand your brand message. Consider the emotions you want to evoke from people and then use fonts which will bring these ideas and emotions to life, as people read your packaging, review your ads, interact with your website and even view your logo.

Brand-Building Touchpoints:

- Different fonts evoke different brand images for your audience.
- The 4 main typography styles are: Serif, Sans Serif, Script, Display.
- The right combination of main fonts, sub/header fonts and accent fonts works together to help you create a compelling brand image which then lives on in people's minds.

Your Brand Is Your Colors

What do your *colors* say about your brand?

Your color selection for your logo, packaging, website and literally everything else is a key element in engineering your brand. Colors can be used to influence people's emotions and behaviors, so there should be ample thought and effort put into finding the right colors to bring your brand to life. The theory of using the right color is integral in all aspects of your branding, such as: building your brand personality, making you stand out from competitors, evoking emotions within people and eliciting strong emotional—and even psychological—responses.

Color is critically important. A study conducted by Satyendra Singh, PhD, found that 90% of impulse purchase decisions were made based on color impressions alone ("Impact of Color on Marketing"). Given this, it's crucial to the overall success of your brand and your business that you select the right color or combination of colors; ones which will make your intended target audience feel exactly what it is you want them to feel. As you've done for each topic covered in this book, think about the types of emotions you want to evoke in people. Decide on potential color selections based on that information. Understanding the psychology of color will help you truly connect with consumers and evoke an appropriate response to your brand. Look at the chart included here to see which emotions are associated with which color choices.

Red	Yellow	Pink	Purple	Green	Blue
Passion	Joy	Feminine	Royal	Safety	Open
Active	Warmth	Creative	Luxury	Balance	Ambitious
Exciting	Positivity	Respect	Creative	Growth	Control
Bold	Happiness	Gratitude	Wise	Generous	Content
Power	Clarity	Softness	Imaginative	Clarity	Spirit
Confidence	Curious	Intuition	Sadness	Prosperity	Trust
Anger	Fun	Calm	Mysterious	Restore	Intellect

Go to the blog on www.EngineerYourBrand.com to find a complete list of meanings for a wide range of colors to find what colors you should use for your brand.

It's important to note that the meanings identified in that image reflect norms in Western society. For different cultures, these colors can hold very different meanings. In Chinese culture, for example, the color red signifies "good luck." If you want your brand to resonate with a large majority of this audience, using red may be a good choice. On the other hand, red is often a sign of "purity" in Indian culture (much the same way white is in Western cultures). Whether you plan to market your product or service specifically to one culture or have future plans to move your product internationally, it's important that you're fully aware of what colors mean to each culture you're communicating with.

In addition to the emotional responses colors create in people, certain colors also affect the physical body. Keep this in mind, particularly if you're thinking of using the following colors to tell your brand story:

- *Red* – increases metabolism, increases respiration rates, raises blood pressure, stimulates appetite

- *Orange* – increases oxygen supply to the brain, produces an invigorating effect, stimulates mental activity
- *Blue* – slows metabolism, produces a calming effect, suppresses appetite, increases both productivity and creativity

If you're aiming to have an upbeat restaurant and decide to paint it blue, that might not be such a great idea. Blue will influence people to remain calm and will reduce their appetites. However, blue might be a good color choice if you own a creative design company and want to create a productive environment, in which people need to arrive at creative solutions to problems.

Color & Packaging

When deciding on the right colors for your product or service, remember that you're likely not the only brand your target audience will see represented in the marketplace. What I mean is, when you're selecting your colors, do be sure they're aligned with your industry. Be careful, though, to not select the exact colors your competitors may be using. If you do, you'll fail to stand out. This is especially true if there's a strong leader within your industry.

If you use colors which are too closely aligned with a clear industry leader, your color selection may actually remind people of the brand or product they already know, trust and are familiar with. That is, your competitor's. Now, if you're trying to create a product that's a clear "Me, too!" item, it could work to your advantage to have a product that looks very similar to the industry leader's.

Test what your color selections look like next to your competitors'. If you have a physical product, bring it in-store and put it beside your competitors'. See if yours stands out or blends in with the crowd, either on a shelf or wherever your brand will be sold. The goal is to make sure that it stands out and that any fonts you've selected are legible against the colors you've chosen. You also want to make sure that your color choice works well with lighting. If your product will be sold in spas for example, it may be displayed in a dark or low-lit space. Opting for dark-colored packaging might not be ideal, since your products may go unnoticed or fail to have the impact you designed them to have.

Other Color Choices

When using color on your website, it's important to ensure that you use colors which blend together well or complement one another. Make sure, too, that your selected colors can be read easily on screen. You don't want to create a site with an all-yellow background that's set it in white type, as this combination is extremely difficult to read. If these are your brand colors, find a way to adapt them for use on your website. Maybe use a white background with black type and then use yellow accent bars to separate various sections of copy.

Once you know what your brand will stand for, I suggest hiring a brand designer to do the design work for you—unless you run a design business yourself. Find a trusted brand and design partner who can then build your color scheme and related brand elements like your logo based on the personality and emotions you're looking to evoke. With this, be careful not to invest in logo or related design services until you know how it is you want people to feel about your brand. Without that, your logo is not the strategic visual mark it could be.

Figure this out first, by establishing a solid brand strategy. You'll then be able to ensure that your color choices match and reinforce your brand personality across everything you do. That bit of advice is worth repeating: Leave the design work for *after* you've done all of your upfront planning. If a designer tells you that prior planning isn't necessary, run the opposite way. Launching into design before you have a clear brand strategy is like setting out on a road trip from Chicago to El Paso … *without a map!*

Brand-Building Touchpoints:

- First and foremost, establish a clear brand strategy.
- Choose colors which bring your brand personality to life.
- Select colors aligned with your target market and industry.
- Be sure your color choices stand out but don't compete with copy.

Your Brand Is Your Name

What does your *name* say about your brand?

Your name is one of the most important aspects of your brand. It's not because the other elements are unimportant. It's because this is what people will refer to you as. This word or phrase will be the vocal representation of your brand and will embody all of its intangible elements. Your brand name is what people say to themselves, when they think about you. It's what they say to others, as they explain their experiences with you. It's also what you say to others, giving them a sense for what your brand stands for and how it can benefit them.

Your brand name makes one of the very first impressions consumers come to associate with you. So, just like selecting a name for a child, the topic of selecting a name for your brand shouldn't be taken lightly. Chances are the brands you love also have great names associated with them. Yes, this is partly because the companies behind them spent lots of upfront time brainstorming and testing several others before they chose what they believe are the perfect names for their brands. Or, maybe, they even hired outside brand strategists or naming agencies to take on this important task. Regardless of how they got there, the end results stick.

Nike doesn't just *sound* cool. Its name was carefully selected to connect consumers with the brand it was seeking to create. Named after the Greek goddess Nike, who personified "victory," it's no accident that the shoe brand embodies this concept. Nor is it a coincidence that Amazon®, the world's largest online retailer, chose to align its name with the Amazon rainforest. The world's largest tropical rainforest is home to an incredibly diverse range of plants, animals and insects which feed into the entire planet's ecosystem. Similarly, Amazon.com offers an incredibly diverse selection of products. Home to everything and anything people could ever want or need, it feeds desires and fuels the global economy.

There are some common rules for arriving at the perfect name and multiple ways to achieve that. The process will vary depending on your industry, what you offer and how your competitors are positioning themselves. Still, there are four types of names and each has its own benefits:

- Descriptive
- Related
- Ambiguous
- Family

Descriptive Names

Descriptive names will, in some way, describe your product, your service, your industry or the solution you provide. These are great for when you want to share exactly what you do with people, using highly direct and simple terms. Descriptive names help consumers instantly recognize your brand's benefits and understand how it plays a direct role in their lives. Examples of descriptive names include:

- Blissful Bath Bombs
- Canada Computers
- Coaching Corner
- M.A.C. Cosmetics
- Leadpages®

While it's tempting to simply say exactly what you do, such as Jack's Automotive, it's important to think about a deeper connection you can make with consumers or added meaning you can hold for people here. What are you really offering them and what do you really do for them? Is there a way to tie an emotion into what you offer or to convey a deeper sense for what your brand delivers? If so, build that into your descriptive brand name.

Think of Whole Foods grocery stores, which offer primarily organic, free trade, whole and healthy foods. The name is descriptive of what they offer without overtly saying "Get your healthy groceries here!" Now, think about how you can describe what you offer—at its core—and make stronger connections with people versus plainly describe what it is you do.

Related Names

Related names are similar to descriptive names, though they sometimes border on being a bit ambiguous. These names are connected to what you offer, what you sell or what you do. However, they do that in less functional ways than descriptive names do. This is where you really need to think about what you offer, the many ways you can say that and the different words you'd like to have associated with your product or service. Get creative and dig into your brand's meaning on both the functional and emotional levels.

Since related names have deeper meanings tied to them, they can truly help form and propel your entire brand. Once people recognize the connection you've made between your brand name and your brand, as a whole, the two become inseparable for them. Review the list of great company names below and the way they convey something more about their brands:

- Nike – named after the Greek goddess who personified "victory"
- Tesla Inc. – named after engineer, physicist and futurist Nikola Tesla, who's best known for contributing to the design of modern A/C electricity supply systems
- Zappos® – a made-up name derived from *zapatos* (Spanish for "shoes")

With these sorts of names, it's helpful to first list out all of the related areas your brand touches. Then, think of ways and words you can use to describe this. It's okay to go way off from what your core offerings are here. Instead, this is where you should really embrace the notion that no idea is a bad idea. These are my favorite names to create for brands!

Ambiguous Names

Completely made-up, or ambiguous, names can also give people a sense for your brand. Ambiguous names still show a connection to your brand, though sometimes the path is less clear. The great thing about these names is that, when people hear or use them, you're in control of the image that comes to mind. Oftentimes they incorporate the names of people, places or things which (on their surface) seem completely unrelated to the company itself.

Either partially or totally ambiguous, popular names in this category include:

- Starbucks® – named after the First Mate of the ship Pequod in *Moby Dick*
- Zoho® – fabricated name given to a customer relationship management tool

When done right, these can be extremely powerful. Ambiguous names can be mashups of various descriptive words which explain what your company's all about. They can represent a combination of initials taken from the names of company partners. They can convey a bit about what your company stands for. Or they can derive from pop culture and literary references.

Family Names

Family names are also where a lot of brand names come from. If you're a coach or have a service-based company, this may be a good type of brand name to use. That's because, in most cases, people are buying "you." If you plan to be the face of your brand throughout the life of your business, having your name connected to it is a great way to demonstrate this. If you do decide to use a family name, also use a tagline which tells people what it is you offer. This will help people connect with you—by connecting the two thoughts, in their minds—right away. We'll dig into the topic of taglines in the next chapter.

Ways to Test Your Name

Once you've created a list of potential names for your brand, you'll want to make sure that your top picks have the greatest chance for success with consumers. Below are five ways I recommend testing your selections to evaluate their suitability as possible names selections:

- Can people say your name properly?
- Does it translate well in other languages?
- Can you claim legal rights to that brand name?

- How does it sound when you use it in a sentence?
- Will it last beyond this season, this year or this century?

First, can people say your brand name properly? Make sure your name can be pronounced as you intend it to be pronounced. People may not always say things the same way or read things in quite the same way. If you think the pronunciation of your name may be misconstrued, ask yourself if you're okay with that. Run through all possible mispronunciations, as well, to get a sense for how your name might sound when it comes out of people's mouths.

Next, how does it translate? If you're planning to expand into other markets, research your name to see how it will translate in other languages which are used by consumers in your intended market(s). There could be a direct translation or several indirect ones. Find out what the name means long before you start printing out business cards or promoting your website. You don't want to assume that your English name will work everywhere, because it won't.

Third, can you own it? You want a name that can be uniquely yours. Make sure to search both the trademark availability of your brand name and its domain name availability. This is necessary from a legal perspective. Most municipalities provide a way to conduct a free name search. Alternately, you can simply google "trademark search" along with your county, state and/or country name to check on the name's availability.

Fourth, how does your brand name sound when it's used in a sentence? Make sure it flows off the tongue well and works seamlessly with surrounding copy. It should also look good in print, on your website and when read using a mobile device. The last thing you want is for your name to look or read oddly on paper, on packaging labels, etc. It can be tricky, also, when your name is closely related to a slang term or similar-sounding word. So, remember not to look at your brand name in isolation. Look at it in the broadest context possible.

Fifth, will it last? Can your brand name stand the test of time? A brand name is something that is rarely changed. If it is changed, it's often a costly and time-consuming process. Save yourself some money and a load of hassle, by making sure you minimize any possibility that yours will go out of style. Avoid names which may seem to be on-trend right now but will likely fade out in a season or two. Ideally, you want your name to be useful to you as long as your business is in operation. For your sake, I hope that's well beyond this season, this year or even this century!

Naming is an aspect of branding that really is both an art and a science. It's not something you're likely to nail by sitting down and thinking about it for an hour or so. It's something you will want to work on over the course of a few days, weeks or even months. You'll want to evaluate and refine your name selections repeatedly. Test the possibilities out on other people. See what they look like on a package sample. Create mock ads to get an idea of how they'll read in print.

Get creative and consider all the various names you could use. Write out a long list of could-be names inspired by any number of things. Put a few different spins on your naming styles before reviewing and cutting away the ones which simply won't work. And, of course, there are naming specialists out there who can do this for you. Have other people build your brand for you, as needed, so you can focus on building your business.

Select a name that embodies your brand, for consumers, and you're one step closer to success!

Brand-Building Touchpoints:

- Naming your brand should not be taken lightly.
- Brainstorm, brainstorm, brainstorm. Then do it again.
- The 4 brand name types are: Descriptive, Related, Ambiguous, Family.
- When selecting your final name, consider: its pronunciation, possible translations, uniqueness, potential uses, appearance and staying power.

Your Brand Is Your Tagline

What does your *tagline* say about your brand?

Quick! Describe your brand in a single sentence. This simple and pointed line is, in essence, your brand tagline. A tagline is typically used alongside your logo and helps consumers sum up who you are and what you do. This one line or statement will also sum up everything else you do from a branding perspective. Sounds easy, right? Just find that one, single line which communicates—in a compelling way—who you are and why that's important to everyone you serve and you're done.

It's about as easy as finding the perfect brand name isn't it? Yet, just like your brand name, your perfect tagline will pay off. As I'm sure you realize, your brand can likely be summed up in many different ways. Because of this, your chances of arriving at the right tagline will be a process that takes time and will require you to look at your brand from a number of different angles. Like your brand name, it's a good idea to create a long list of all the different ways your brand could be described.

Make It Simple

To get you started, here are a few angles to look at when building out your tagline:

- What do you do for your customers or the community?
- What functional benefits does your brand offer consumers?
- How do/will your products or services make consumers feel?

- Which one, focused idea do you want your brand to stand for?

List out a variety of sentences or statements which might sum up your brand, using the above ways of reflecting to inform your list. Jot down all possible ideas for how you can describe your brand, giving yourself options which can then be translated into your tagline.

Simplicity is a winning formula for taglines. You want people to easily take away why your brand is important and why it's important to their lives. If it isn't easily remembered or easily shared, then your tagline won't serve its purpose of helping crystalize your brand in people's minds. You want consumers to read your tagline and instantly understand what it is you offer them. If you try to be too clever or cheeky with it, you risk making your audience think too hard about this statement and having it go completely over their heads, in which case it's lost on them.

Focus Is Key

The tagline you ultimately decide on should be focused. I know you want to tell people all of the amazing things you do and why they should buy your product or service. But, if you try to have people take away too many things, they won't take away anything at all. Focus on the one thing you want people to know you stand for and the one thing that will make you connect with your consumer. Then, try to stay in that territory. Think about what you offer which no one else does, translating this into a pithy statement people will then relate back to you. There shouldn't be any competing ideas here—because you're staying focused, right?

There shouldn't be any industry jargon involved, either. Use plain English to create a statement which helps end users understand you and your offerings clearly. A good way to achieve this is by using what I call the 8/88

Test. That is, how would you describe what you offer to both an 8-year old and an 88-year old? I know, as you do, that there are many extremely intelligent 8-year olds and a lot of very sharp 88-year olds out there. Still, use the 8/88 Test to gauge the simplicity of your statement. If neither a child nor a grandparent understands what you're trying to tell them with a particular tagline, go back to the drawing board.

Whatever statement you use, you should be able to share it with anyone and they should more or less get what it is you do. The goal is simply to make sure they understand what you're trying to say. To get a sense for the breadth of the tagline routes available to you, see the examples below. They include a wide range of options:

- *Think Different.* – This truly embodies everything Apple, which has revolutionized and entrenched the conventions for many of the markets it competes in.
- *Just Do It.* – This statement perfectly sums up the empowerment Nike seeks to instil.
- *You're Richer than You Think.* This Scotiabank® tagline showcases how the right guidance can help you save money and make more money than you thought possible.
- *... Where You Go to See What's Happening Everywhere in the World Right Now.* – Ironically, the tagline for Twitter® is quite long compared to the others. However, it does capture the essence of what it does and why people want to be on its platform.
- *Where Businesses Thrive.* – The tagline for the WeWork® global shared office space highlights the benefits small businesses experience when they transition to a co-working space.

Like all aspects of your brand, ideally you should create your tagline so that it does not need to be changed frequently nor be changed drastically over time.

Revisit It Now & Then

Since your brand is a long-term and long-living asset, you'll want your tagline to stay true to your brand. Over time, your business may be affected by shifts in your target market. When this happens, you'll want to revisit your tagline to ensure that it continues to connect with your intended audience. There are two main reasons your tagline may need to be revised, where changes in your target audience are concerned.

First, you may want your brand to grow alongside your target audience. As its members experience new life stages, your brand message will need to shift slightly to continue to connect with them. Speaking to someone during their youthful years and then during their early parenting years will likely require a change in messaging. In turn, your tagline may need to evolve here. Second, if you're continuously speaking to one age group, this group's needs may change over time. This can be especially true if you're speaking to a young audience over a long period and you need to constantly stay relevant.

Take Coca-Cola, which targets a young audience and has had 46 different taglines over the course of its 130-plus-year lifespan. While its tagline from 1886 "Delicious and Refreshing" would still make sense today, that's much more functional than today's emotional tagline "Taste the Feeling". This evolution shows a transition from a mere functional description to a more emotional one. This is based on a change in times and overall evolution of the brand.

By contrast, Nike has used the "Just Do It" tagline since its 1988 inception. This statement is as relevant and strong today as it's ever been. Your own tagline can come from what you do, what you offer or how you make people feel. Yet, regardless of how you arrive at this statement, it must mean something to you and to your customer—today and, hopefully, for years to come. You want people to read this message, immediately understand your brand, know who you are and have an idea of why your brand is the right fit for them.

Brand-Building Touchpoints:

- Your tagline should be short, direct and sum up your brand.
- It can be based on functional benefits, emotional benefits or ideas.
- Use the 8/88 Test: Does your tagline make sense to both an 8 and 88-year old?

Your Brand Is Your Advertising

What does your *advertising* say about your brand?

Connecting with the right people, in the right places and with the right messages is your branding effort brought to life through advertising. The time to start thinking about how you'll tell people about what you offer is after you have the other elements of your brand we've discussed, thus far, laid out: What you will sell, where it will be sold, what price you'll charge, what it will look like, which colors you'll use, etc.

Where you decide to connect with your audience, how often you connect with it and what messaging you'll use all add up to your advertising—a crucial element to engineering your brand. How you go about advertising will vary, depending on your unique brand. Just as your product is uniquely yours, your advertising plan will also be unique yours. There's no one-size-fits-all for advertising. There's simply what fits for your brand (and what doesn't).

When building the right advertising plan, you'll want to take into consideration where your consumers are and where your competitors are. Namely, where do members of your target audience spend their time? Do they watch lots of home renovation shows? If so, are they accessing them through traditional TV or online streaming services? Do they listen to podcasts? If so, which sorts of podcasts do they listen to? Are they spending hours on Instagram® or LinkedIn®? If so, why? Or are they reading blogs and magazine articles? If so, which ones?

Your Advertising Options

Knowing where your audience is will help you understand where it makes sense to both promote your brand and share information about it with them. The more you understand this the better chance you have of getting your brand message heard by your selected audience. There are a wide range of places your target audience may be spending its time. Your goal, as it relates to consumer interaction with specific advertising channels, is to find out exactly: where your best customers are, at what times of day, on which days of the week and what messages they're most open to receiving.

Review the following list of possible advertising channels your target audience may be spending time with. Identify the ones you might use, in order to speak directly to your best customers:

On Screen	Social Media
• Commercials (i.e., TV, online, in-theatre) • Product Placement (your product used in a live program or show) • Search Engine Ads • Website or Blogsite Ads	• Facebook • Instagram • LinkedIn • Pinterest • Snapchat® • Twitter • YouTube® • -&- others

On Air	Live Events
<ul><li>Radio or Podcast Ads</li><li>Radio or Podcast Sponsorship or Interviews</li><li>Unique Playlists (Think: Household cleaning tips on Spotify® "… brought to you by Mr. Clean®")</li></ul>	<ul><li>Conferences & Tradeshows</li><li>Courses, Retreats, Workshops</li><li>Networking Events</li><li>Product Sampling or Pop-Ups</li><li>Speaking Engagements</li></ul>
Sponsors/Influencers	**Print**
<ul><li>Affiliates (who receive a % of sales closed when followers use a special link)</li><li>Online Influencers (who share your product/service info with their followers)</li><li>Special Events & Giveaways</li><li>Team, Nonprofit or Event Sponsorship</li></ul>	<ul><li>Billboard Ads</li><li>Business Flyers</li><li>Direct Mailers</li><li>Newspaper Ads</li><li>Magazine Ads</li><li>Transit Ads</li></ul>
Written Content	**Person-to-Person Connection**
<ul><li>Books & e-Books</li><li>Company Websites or Blog Articles</li><li>Third-Party Websites or Blog Articles</li></ul>	<ul><li>Cold Calls</li><li>Emails & e-Newsletters</li><li>Webinars</li></ul>

These are just a few examples of the various ways you can promote your business, as covering the full range (or each one, in detail) would require an entirely separate book. Use these thought starters to imagine the advertising channels available to you when you begin to connect with your target audience. Get curious and find out where your best customers are, as this will guide you to the sorts of channels you should be using. Stay true to where your brand would be, if it were a person, using related advertising channels to successfully build out a strategy that communicates "who" your brand is and who it's intended for.

Not only is it important to understand where your audience is spending its time. You also want to understand why people are spending their time interacting with these channels of communication. Said differently, what problems are they trying to solve by engaging with them? Does your audience go to YouTube for tutorials and then to Pinterest for inspiration? Do they watch TV as a way to escape or as a way to educate themselves? Are they reading magazines for motivation or for information? Understanding why people are drawn to any specific advertising channels you aim to use will ensure that you speak directly to them, in ways which have the best chance of connecting with them along those channels.

Competitor Messaging

The key with every branding effort you invest time and money in is to create a unique voice for your brand—and your brand only. While building your brand through advertising, you can do this by either using different channels than your competitors or by using different messaging from your competitors. I recommend doing a bit of both. Now, I understand that you can't be in completely different channels from your competitors all the time. After all, you're trying to reach the same people. However, you can separate yourself from your competitors by reaching out to your target audience in new and different ways.

Let's say a competitor promotes their brand through a YouTube Influencer who has 1 Million followers. Perhaps you can get multiple YouTube Influencers with 50,000 followers each to promote your product. If everyone in your industry is running print ads, maybe you can run an Advertorial (or editorial-style ad) instead. Or, while everyone else is busy conducting webinars, why not host a live workshop for people? You want to capture your audience's attention when and where other people aren't doing likewise. So, spend time thinking of ways you can reach your audience which others have overlooked or are ignoring altogether.

Your Messaging

Once you've selected where you should advertise—based on where you consumer is and where your competitors are not—decide on what message you want to send with your advertising. Your goal is to end up with clear, concise messaging that highlights who your brand is and how it connects to your audience. The work you've done in earlier chapters will certainly help with this.

In particular, I suggest referring back to Chapter 1 ("Your Brand Is Your Purpose") and Chapter 6 ("Your Brand Is the Language You Use"). They'll help you reconnect with your purpose and weigh your word choice carefully, as you develop key messaging for your advertising materials. That way your message will connect with your audience and bring your unique brand voice to life, as you speak to topics of importance to your individual brand and to your customer base.

By also understanding why and when people may see, hear or otherwise interact with your ads, you can tailor your messaging to suit the specific needs your audience is experiencing when it comes across your brand in the selected channel. Just like a human being, your brand is multi-dimensional and complex. You can and should communicate different things on different channels and at different times of day. Put yourself in your audience's shoes and ask, "How can my brand create value for these people at this *exact* moment?" What they want to hear on their ride into work is different from what they want to read on a Saturday morning or watch on YouTube on a Thursday night.

In advertising messages, specifically, it's helpful to speak to either a pain point or a soft spot your audience holds. Let's say you represent Bissell® vacuums and are about to create messaging for the brand. Maybe you know that a soft spot for the typical Bissell owner is that they just love their cats so much that they let them sleep on whichever couches and chairs they want to. Along with this, you'd also know that a pain point for these consumers is the difficulty involved in getting that cat hair off of the couches and chairs their beloved cat, let's call it Boots, rolls around on all day.

Given this, you'd create a message that speaks directly to those two points: 1.) We know you love your cat Boots, and, 2.) We know vacuuming up Boots' hair can be a challenge. Pair these ideas with your brand personality and you have a winning formula for meaningful advertising copy that connects with your audience! While doing this, stay true to your brand and stay true to the channel you're using. What you say in an email, at a tradeshow or on social media will differ—though the tone and delivery of each of these messages should be similar. Keep in mind where your audience will likely be, as it's taking in your message, and then cater your message to that space.

Again, what someone wants to read on a Saturday morning is different from what it will be at noon on Tuesday. And, certainly, what someone watches on YouTube will be different from what they expect to see during a commercial break on their local weather channel. Advertising should always benefit your audience rather than be a bother. Meeting people where they are, when they're there and providing a timely problem-solving message is a sure way to benefit them.

Advertisements

The imagery contained in your ads plays a crucial role in building your brand. So, when it comes time to use your messaging to develop advertisements, be equally selective about the people, places and things you include from a visual perspective. This applies to the colors and fonts you select to represent your brand, as well as any images of your product, spokesmodels and situations you choose to represent it. When combined together, these pieces serve as visual ads which connect with your audience on whatever channels you've identified as making sense for them and for your brand.

Ask whether illustrative images can adequately bring your brand to life or whether photographs would do a better job. Decide whether it's helpful to show people using your product or whether showing your product by itself is enough. Perhaps your product is well-suited to everyday situations. Maybe an elaborate and exaggerated scenario would amplify the message you're trying to create. Too, do you want to highlight the functional or the emotional benefits your product offers? Play around, trying different variations on each of these strategies. Your brand should dictate a lot of these key image decisions for you. You should then aim to be consistent in how you portray your brand using visual ads.

If you're using real people in your advertising, do your best to select models who represent your brand and its end users. Think about the mid-2000s "Get a Mac" campaign with a young, hip man dressed in a hoodie and jeans showing off a Macintosh computer, saying: "Hello, I'm a Mac." The PC, on the other hand, was represented by a middle-aged man who was slightly overweight, wore a suit that didn't quite fit and appeared to be the stereotypical accountant.

These two images, when contrasted in Apple computer ads, literally personified the two separate brand images to solidify who each brand spoke to and did not speak to. When casting for models or finding the perfect stock images for your own brand, ask if the people they include could represent your brand on their own. If not, keep searching.

Don't forget about the music that accompanies your advertising, either. While you won't need to think of this for many forms of advertising, there are some it makes absolute sense for. The tone of any music you choose will help set the tone for your brand. So, is it upbeat or relaxing? Dramatic or mundane? The sounds and music used in your advertising can be extremely powerful in eliciting emotions from your audience. When properly selected, music and tones can be powerful tools which bring up memories—causing audience members to laugh, cry, smile and/or feel a range of other emotions. Leading people to respond emotionally to your brand is exactly what you want to do.

Finally, where you tell your story should reflect something about what you're saying. This is why selecting the right channels is fundamental to ensuring that your brand has a chance to be seen and/or heard by your specific audience. Advertising brings your brand to life, telling others the story you want to tell them. While having a presence ensures that they see you, being in the right places at the right times ensures that you create the right mental image of your brand. By getting a sense for what people want to hear, when they hear about you on different channels, you increase your probability of connecting with them.

If yours is a crafty brand, be where crafty people hang out and deliver a message that looks and sounds "crafty." If yours is a sporty brand, be where sporty people are—using language they would use to convey a "sporty" feel. Since no target audience is one-dimensional, resist limiting your sporty brand's advertising opportunities to sporting events alone. Imagine a week in the life of an actual person from this group. Yes, they might like to watch Monday night football. It could also be that they shop for groceries on Sunday nights, commute to work by car weekday mornings, tune into A.M. sports radio during their drive, grab a specific brand of coffee to-go on Friday mornings, etc.

The last thing you want is to be an annoyance, by not giving people the messages they want when and where they want them. Instead, your goal is to create value for your audience. That opportunity is lost, if you speak to its members incorrectly or miss them altogether. Similarly, if you're overly obtrusive or negatively impact an enjoyable experience someone may be having, you risk creating a "never" reaction to your brand. No one's happy when an ad interrupts something they're in the middle of. After all, that's not the main attraction.

So, in situations like these, be sure your brand messaging enhances their experience. By creating value, in ways which prove that the user experience is top of mind for your brand, you make it easier for those on the receiving end to get true value out of the brand message you're sharing.

Brand-Building Touchpoints:

- Your brand message should be where your audience is.
- Even if using the same channels, stand out from competitors.
- Select language, images and sounds with your audience in mind.

Your Brand Is Your Strategic Alliances

What do your *strategic alliances* say about your brand?

You are who you surround yourself with. This is as true for brands as it is for people. Who your brand associates with says a lot about your brand itself, who you serve and what you stand for. Surrounding your brand with the right people, other relevant brands and entire organizations allows you to enhance its credibility and solidify its personality, in association with others. Building relationships through partnerships, co-promotions and social responsibility are all important ways you can borrow brand credibility and engineer your brand image.

Depending on your type of business, you may need to immediately establish strategic partnerships with other brands. If you're a third-party who represents and sells other people's products or services, this is especially true. Let's say you own a coffee shop that lacks a large kitchen area, yet you also want to sell pastries and sandwiches. What local bakery will provide these offerings to your patrons? There may be dozens to choose from, so how do you make sure to select the right partnering brand for you? If you own a local outdoor clothing company, which industry brands are the best fit for selling in your store? Viewed another way, which ones will offer your customers the type of outdoor shopping brand experience you're looking to create?

Strategic partnership decisions like these are not to be taken on lightly. In the eyes of consumers, all brands which are connected to your brand and are sold alongside (or under the banner of) your brand are a reflection of who you are and what you stand for. Take the opportunity that partnering with other brands presents to continuously build on the imagery and ideas associated with your own company.

If you know you want to make tea available to visitors of your local craft store, the exact brand of tea you offer is something worth putting extra thought into. Consider what your brand stands for and look for suppliers or potential partners who use similar brand messaging. If you're all about inspiring creativity, a tea that delivers the same message is a far better choice than a familiar or traditional tea brand no matter the cost difference. The long-term benefits of building a strong, consistent brand image is worth more than any immediate savings.

Why Partner Up?

There comes a time, in business, when it truly makes sense for your brand to partner with other brands. This can be anything from partnering with another business on a cross-promotion sale to co-sponsoring a special event with a recognized organization. One reason this may be beneficial is that it can open up opportunities for your brand which you aren't able to secure for yourself, such as when the financial cost of doing something on your own is impractical. Or when you feel that end users would have a better experience, overall, if you were able to offer them something of added value by partnering with another business. While you might be able to give away free samples of your coffee to customers in a retail store, wouldn't shoppers be even more ecstatic to receive a free coffee from you along with a third-party coupon for savings on a reusable mug?

Strategic alliances let you do more for less, while still gaining the positive effects of sponsoring an event or supporting a cause you believe in. Partnering up with like-minded brands can also amplify your own message and help spread the word about what you, as a brand, stand for. As with everything you do for your brand, you want to constantly build up your image. So, partnering with companies or organizations which help you create that image and provide value for end users is a great way to engineer a winning brand.

Just like selecting the right font, selecting the right partner is crucial to building you brand. Imagine you own a luxury chocolate company and you're looking to partner with a beverage company for a private or public event you're hosting. Chocolate pairs nicely with several types of beverages, so your first step is to decide which option will best convey the level of luxury you're looking to evoke with your own brand. You could pair it with tea, coffee, wine, cognac, brandy, whisky or milk—just to name a few! Each of these pairings will portray a different level of luxury. Within each of these beverage categories, there are various brands you could pair with to bring the right level of luxury to your event and, in turn, prospective or existing customers.

Let's say you decide to pair with brandy. Since this smooth and flavor-filled alcohol is rarely paired with other foods, it allows you to create a truly unique experience for your patrons. You then have to decide which exact brandy label will help you build the optimal image of luxury, in the minds of attendees. You could select Hennessey®, St. Remy®, Martell® or a range of available brands. Ultimately, the best choice is to go with the brandy which has a brand image most similar to your own. Luxury can mean many things, so really look at how luxury is conveyed through the brand you'd like to work with. The one you select should offer the same level of luxury you're looking to establish through your chocolate brand.

In addition, use your potential partner brand's strengths to make up for any shortcomings you may have. Continuing with the chocolate example, let's say yours is a new luxury chocolate brand and you're trying to instill awareness in your select target audience. It might be beneficial for you to partner with a brandy that's already established as being in the luxury space. Existing credibility with the target audience you're also hoping to attract will lend itself to you, in turn helping you build your brand image and position yourself as occupying the same space as an entrenched brand that's done a lot of the hard work already. That kind of partnership allows your brand to snuggle right up beside the positive sentiments people already hold about a brand they know and presumably love.

People & Organizations as Partners

Partners to your brand can also be people who speak about your brand on your behalf. Today, we mostly refer to these as "influencers," although celebrity endorsements are the same thing. These are people who will use your product or service and then share their experiences through images or stories about what it was like to interact with your brand. Because these people already have followings and are considered authority figures by their followers, this is a great way to grow your brand through positive connections. You can either align your brand with influencers or celebrities whom you genuinely believe would benefit from it or with those who are benefiting from it already—using their recognition of your product or service to amplify your credibility.

Engineering your brand through sponsorships is another way to build your brand through association. A sponsorship is when you pay to have your brand name or logo associated with an event, person or organization. The same holds true for products and services. Will sponsoring an event that's aligned with your brand identity help you build the associations you want to build in consumers' minds? Just like deciding which types of stores you want your brand to appear in, you also want to be selective about any events, individuals or organizations you sponsor or partner with.

Going back to our luxury chocolate example, it wouldn't make much sense for this brand to sponsor a children's sports team. Nor an adult sports team, for that matter. It'd make sense for it to sponsor an Ice Wine Festival, though!

If you're considering sponsorship of any kind, the following questions will help you determine if a particular pairing is right for your brand:

- Would my target audience be delighted by it?
- Will it deliver added value for my target audience?
- Is there a clear connection to my brand's core values?
- Will the partnership bring to life more than just my logo?
- Are his/her/its personality traits similar to those of my brand?

No matter how much you want to support an athlete, a cause or an event, it won't always make sense to do so when building your brand. With events, specifically, consider who's likely to attend and what image the event presents before sponsoring it.

Your Brand & Social Responsibility

How and where does your brand show support for its community, if at all? Another primary way to engineer your brand through associations is by setting up a corporate or brand social responsibility program, aligning your brand with a charity or a cause. This is more important today than ever, as consumers now expect organizations to give back.

The good news, for you, is that consumers think more favorably of brands, which demonstrate a level of social responsibility and, therefore, put a premium on these brands. According to a 2014 Nielsen® global research study, 55% of respondents said they'd be willing to pay more for goods which reflect a commitment to corporate social responsibility. Partnerships like these are not only a great way to show people who's behind your brand and what it stands for. They also show that giving back to communities which actively support your brand matters to you.

When you're deciding what type of cause makes sense for your business, think about what's important to your customers and to you. Ideally, what makes sense for your business brand and for you, as a business owner, is aligned somewhat. If not, then I urge you to align your brand with a charity or cause that does make sense for your business. While I know you may be able to make a stronger contribution by having donations and efforts come directly from your company, you're still making a business decision. So, don't let your heart get the best of you.

When I worked for Campbell's Soup, for a time I managed all of its corporate social responsibility (CSR) initiatives across Canada. This was an assignment I absolutely loved, felt truly connected to and was proud of. While being on-boarded, I learned about all of the different CSR initiatives the company had launched. That's when it became clear to me that one of the initiatives just didn't make sense.

You see, Campbell's stands strongly behind the cause of hunger alleviation. The brand regularly donates to food banks, holds internal food drives and encourages employees to donate time at those food banks—where they then gladly sort and stack incoming food items. Given that and the fact that it offers low-cost meal options for many families, it makes perfect sense for the company to support hunger alleviation. What didn't make sense to me was a program that had no connection to alleviating hunger.

The program allowed groups, which were mostly school-based, to collect labels from various Campbell's products and then redeem them for tangible items. Since the majority of people using the program were affiliated with schools, the majority of the items those labels could be redeemed for were school-related. Think basketballs, crayons, jump ropes and trumpets. Now, don't get me wrong. I do believe that children and schools need support, but I couldn't—for the life of me—see how this was connected to Campbell's Soup! Needless to say, this program is no longer categorized as a CSR initiative for the company.

The charities or causes you donate to should be extensions of your brand and may even become so engrained in your brand that people begin to associate you and your cause together. TOMS® Shoes is famously known as The One for One Company. The purchase of any pair of shoes from this brand leads to the donation of a pair of shoes to someone less fortunate. This program has been so successful that people will buy TOMS footwear solely because they know that others will benefit from their purchases. This is their brand. Their brand stands for "giving."

Your company doesn't need to adopt an extreme giving program, like TOMS does, but you should consider what other people will think of your brand's charitable contributions. That includes people outside of your organization and people within your organization. Will your own social responsibility program strengthen the image you're building for your company, when it comes to how customers and employees will perceive it? Or will it leave them scratching their heads, the way I did when faced with the label-collection program at Campbell's? CSR is a means for strengthening people's understanding of your brand, reinforcing its core values and being viewed as unique by all who come in contact with it.

When considering or selecting strategic alliances for your business, remember that anything and anyone your brand connects with then builds your brand in some way. It's easy to want to partner with a person or organization that'll help drive sales in the short run. Yet, when you think about the long-term effects of confusing your consumers, the short-term payoff certainly isn't worth it. Your brand is your most important asset and you must treat it as such.

Lastly, as tough as this may sound, be sure your soft spot doesn't get the best of you when aligning your brand with a charity or cause. It sounds a bit harsh, I know, but the brand you align yourself with is meant to assist with your own brand-building process—not only make you feel warm and fuzzy. You should absolutely align your business with a charity or cause that makes sense for your business. That won't necessarily be your kid's hockey team, the local pet store or a nearby women's shelter unless any of these align with your brand. And, hey, they might! All I'm saying is be sure to find an angle that makes sense for your brand and that helps you protect your most valuable asset.

Brand-Building Touchpoints:

- Build your brand in association with other brands, people or organizations.
- If you're selling other brands under yours, be sure they build your image.
- Select partnerships or sponsorships which align well with your brand.
- When it comes to alliances, avoid letting your heart rule your head.

Your Brand Is Your Loyalty Offerings

What do your *loyalty offerings* say about your brand?

Do you give people added reasons to love your brand? That's basically what building your brand through loyalty offers is. It's giving people more reason to love your specific brand. You've done everything else right, getting customers to buy from you. Now you have an opportunity to reward them for buying from you versus anyone else. So, how can you sweeten the deal and keep customers coming back for more?

Remember, your competitors are also trying to win their hearts and wallets—just as you are—and they won't stop simply because you've beat them at securing one or two sales. Strengthening your brand through loyalty offerings will help you build long-term success with your customers and your overall business. There's another reason to keep your customers happy by engineering a successful loyalty program for them: It's more expensive to gain a new client than to simply have an existing client buy more from you and/or buy from you more often.

Your current customers already know you, have a relationship with you and, hopefully, trust you. By becoming a valuable fixture in their regular routines, you can learn more about your business through them, grow your customer base through them and help them evolve into brand ambassadors. Yet, how you reward your customers is just as important as what you reward them with. What that looks like will depend on your brand and your particular brand of customer.

Keep 'Em Coming Back

There are numerous ways to reward people for being (or becoming) loyal customers. The trick is in choosing a reward system that works well for them and connects them to your brand without eroding your brand value. Consider the many different loyalty experiences you likely encounter. Maybe you carry around a frequent diner punch card for a local restaurant. Or have something on your keychain you scan at your local gym to earn personal training or juice bar credits. You might automatically earn points at checkout when you shop with an online retailer or even use an app on your phone to earn free drinks from your local coffee shop. All of these do the same thing, though they say completely different things about the brands behind them.

Think about what's already been helpful, in building your brand for your audience, and then build on that concept. For me, taking out my wallet and finding whatever loyalty card is needed for wherever I am is far less motivating than pulling out my phone and quickly scanning a code—or simply using a plastic keychain tab to earn rewards. However, if you're launching a nostalgic coffee shop in which people expect your brand to give them a taste of "how things used to be" and/or your frequent customers would find it easier to do business with you, using a paper loyalty card and ink stamp system may be the best approach.

Here are some different methods you can use to set up a loyalty system with customers:

- A branded retail store app
- A branded loyalty points card
- A frequent shopper punch card

Once you decide how people can best take advantage of your loyalty offerings, you then have to decide on how you can motivate them to connect with you and be rewarded for coming back time and again. It's clear why you want them back. But, is it clear to your customers that they should come back—and do it often? A few of the special perks you can offer consumers, as you engineer your brand into one they choose to be loyal to, include:

- $ OFF or % OFF savings
- Early access to new releases
- Free products and/or gift items
- Exclusive, limited-time or mystery deals
- Invites to Meet & Greets, parties, trunk shows, etc.

There really are countless ways to reward people for shopping with you over and over again. Think about what would surprise and delight your customers and find ways to give them just that.

A local coffee shop I go to, while in Toronto, has converted many of its customers into loyal followers by creating a unique, brand-related experience for their coffee-loving audience. This coffee shop has a strong following in the city. So much so that it sells shirts, hats and mugs with its logo on it. People all across the city use these items with pride. Since this shop attracts devotees of all kinds, it's tiered its rewards based on what makes sense for different patron segments.

Its first tier of loyalty rewards is similar to that of most other coffee shops: a FREE brewed coffee. Following that, at the next points tier, is a FREE food or specialty drink item. Next comes a FREE bag of coffee to take home. Then a FREE mug. The top tier patron, who comes into the shop religiously day after day, is offered an altogether unique reward—a trip to the coffee roaster! For a true coffee lover, this is a pretty cool experience that's worth saving up loyalty points for. Even if no one ever redeems it, the idea that this coffee shop offers an experience that connects with true coffee lovers is what makes it a great solution for building its brand and getting people excited.

What would your own audience love to receive from you, in the form of a reward that connects it to your business? Use that to build your brand, letting it speak to what you stand for, what you offer and how what you do matters to those individuals on a deeper level. Get creative here. If you own a yoga studio, maybe you offer a free kombucha drink after eight visits. If you run a designer women's clothing store, maybe you throw free makeover parties for guests who've spent a certain amount of money with you. Even artists like Taylor Swift use loyalty programs to build their brands. Swift is famously known for throwing massive release parties at her home, inviting some of her top fans. What a way to reward loyalty and build brand love! When you surprise and delight your customers with rewards they really want, they will reward you with their loyalty over time.

When you're talking about the levels people are at with their rewards, make sure this ties into your brand. Defining your rewards simply Level 1, Level 2 and Level 3 is a lost opportunity to create a connection with your audience. The same goes for Gold, Silver and Platinum reward levels. None of them mean very much, do they? Think about what makes sense for you and your business. If you own a coffee shop, you might name your levels: Caffeinated, Buzzed and Watch Out World, Here I Come! By naming your tiers or levels in ways which reflect your brand, you instantly bring it to life and showcase what it is, what it stands for and what it means to others.

Treat Your Best the Best

Not all customers are created equal. Given this, not all customers should be treated equally. The person who spends $200 a month with you and the person who spends $2,000 a month with you are not equal, so don't treat them as if they are. You'd need to attract ten of the first to make up for one lost sale with the second, so taking better care of the $2,000 customer is vital for your business and brand success!

I'm not saying you shouldn't treat all customers well. I'm just saying you should aim to treat your high-value customers slightly better. Yes, even when it comes to loyalty rewards. Offer everyone a great experience and rewards which are brand-specific, but reserve amazing or unforgettable rewards for your highest paying customers. Let's say you provide a percentage off merchandise after customers have completed so many transactions with you. The savings you offer top-tier customers should be greater than those you offer lower-tier customers. That's one way to thank the first group, which plays a greater role in helping you sustain and grow your brand, and to create stronger bonds with the people who comprise it.

Perhaps, instead, you do something uniquely special for your best customers. That something, from their perspective, then serves to elevate your brand even more. If you're a service company, you might want to take those customers golfing, reward them with spa treatments, give them tickets to concerts/shows or provide them with free, exclusive consultations. Whatever you can do to make them love you even more, do it! Don't risk losing these ever-important customers.

Make Sharing Easy & They'll Do It

People share what they love—and what they're asked to share. If you invite someone to share comments about their experience with you or a purchase they just made, they might actually do so. If you reward them for taking this action, they're far more likely to do it. This is another form of driving loyalty that oftentimes gets overlooked. This is a great way to grow your brand, since this strategy can be extremely impactful.

If you have 10 people share word of your business with just 1 friend each, all of a sudden you've *doubled* the number of people who are aware of and exposed to your brand. If those 10 additional people then share your message with 1 person each, you'll have *tripled* the effect. Think of the exponential growth opportunities for your brand, which are generated by asking someone to share your brand with others. Reward people for sharing the good word and you'll be amazed by how much marketing they do for you and by how many sales they generate for your brand, when all you had to do was ask.

Rewarding customers for being loyal to you will both build your brand and increase brand love among your customers. How you do this will differ based on what your brand offers, how you go about getting them excited about what it stands for and how well you communicate that their business is important to you. Although not all customers are the same, you can reward everyone for their patronage at some level. Still, you want to make sure to take extra special care of your top-tier customers, so that they keep coming back to you time and time again.

Brand-Building Touchpoints:

- Offer the right rewards for your customers.
- Be creative, connecting your rewards to your brand.
- Reward your best customers even more, showing that you value them.
- Ask people to share your brand on your behalf and reward them for doing so.

Your Brand Is Consistency

What does *consistency* say about your brand?

Consistency is the true secret to how you build a brand. And, when it comes to brands, people love the expected. If you fail to be consistent in what your brand stands for and how it connects with people, your clients won't know what to think of you. They won't know who you are, they won't know what you stand for and, most importantly, they won't know how you can help them. We've been taught that people love the unexpected in life—and this is true for some things: a spontaneous trip to the Bahamas, a special dish on your favorite restaurant's menu or the sudden rush of amazing feelings you experience when you go bungee jumping for the first time.

These types of unexpected moments are absolutely craved, needed and enjoyed in life. When it comes to what people want from their brands, however, they absolutely crave, need and demand consistency. This doesn't mean you can't be creative or should resist rolling out new products, special offers or unusual experiences. What it does mean is that you need to consistently deliver the same image and provide the same look and feel across everything your brand does. People should feel the same emotions (or connection) to your brand after they visit your website, have a product delivered to their door, talk to you on the phone or engage in any other touchpoint with you. This type of consistency is what consumers want and it's the key to your success.

People have enough to think about in their day-to-day lives. What's the weather like? What's going to happen at work today? Will the kids eat their vegetables at dinner tonight? Let alone the big, unexpected things people have to deal with. They don't want to have to think about how a brand will make them feel. They want to know exactly how it will make them feel. A consistent image, if it's right for your consumers, is what draws them back to you. They want you to be a reliable part of their lives, so they can avoid making yet another decision. Through consistency, they know (for once) what they're getting in their day: Your brand serves as a *relief* to them.

How Our Brains Work

Let's talk about why people want consistency from their brands to show you how extremely important this really is. To truly understand this, we must first come to terms with the fact that humans are not a terribly evolved species. I mean, yes, we have gone to the Moon and are making our way to Mars. Yes, your intellect makes it easy for you to read the words on this page. Yes, there have been amazing discoveries throughout time which help define our species.

Overall, though, we haven't evolved much in the last 500,000 years. Our minds still work quite a lot like our primitive ancestors' did. Because we haven't evolved all that much, our minds still function much like they did when we were more animalistic. What that translates to is the fact that we're inherently programmed to conserve energy, just as our hunter/gatherer ancestors were. They had to be on constant alert for predators and scavenge for food, since they couldn't store it the way we do today. That lingering, energy-conserving mentality also drives us to take the path of least resistance and to rely on past experience, so that we can wisely assess future outcomes when we make decisions.

From our ancestors' perspectives, that meant going to the same tree every day; the one most likely to have the best and most easily accessible fruit hanging from it. It meant walking the most efficient route to gather water; the one that was quickest, easiest and made us least detectable to predators. From today's human perspective, if all past data points tell me that Skittles® is a fun brand, tastes great, fills me up and provides an element of play, that's what I'll expect from all of my future interactions with Skittles. If I see an ad for the candy which doesn't have an element of play in it or its packaging suddenly portrays seriousness versus playfulness, I'll feel like something isn't quite right and my mind won't like it one bit.

It'd be the same for our ancestor who goes to her favorite plum tree to enjoy some fresh, ripe, juicy plums. Only the tree's now filled with bananas! All of a sudden her brain doesn't know how to categorize this experience and gets confused—and a confused mind is *never* good for business. What was supposed to be a simple decision, whether it's getting a juicy plum or buying a bag of candy, requires extra work and taxes our systems. This results in an unconscious, negative reaction to the brand in question which then creates a negative association with that brand. Our minds tell us (on a subconscious level) that it's not easy to deal with. Therefore, it must not be a very good choice. Our minds then convince us to choose something we know we can trust, like a more consistently branded competitor product or service.

Let Science Be Your Guide

There's a famous saying in neuroscience: "Neurons that fire together wire together." Translation? When two activities "fire" or happen at the same time, the bond between these two actions grows stronger and stronger with every occurrence. This is why habits are difficult to break.

If for 20 years you've come home after work and watched TV and now instead want to start running two miles as soon as you get home, your body and mind will kick up resistance to this. The "coming home from work" neurons and the "watching TV" neurons have been trained to fire together, working hand-in-hand to forge a path of least resistance in your mind. Your mind then compels you to continue taking these actions in tandem, because that's what it's been trained to do. Likewise, if we repeatedly get a sense of happiness from drinking Coca-Cola and our brains consistently deliver a feeling of euphoria when we do so, it makes us want to choose Coca-Cola over and over again whenever we're looking for a pick-me-up.

Put science to work for the benefit of your own brand, making it the path of least resistance for new and existing customers. You want the emotions you evoke in your target audience to be consistent, so that your product or service and the emotions you want to elicit with it become wired together. When you deliver the same experience over and over again, consumers won't need to think about making decisions anymore. They'll only need to know that your product or service repeatedly makes them feel a certain way. Anytime they want to recreate that feeling, going to you is a sure way to deliver on this sensation and get their needs met.

They can just go to the shelf, pick up your brand, pay for it and enjoy your product—without thinking twice or ever considering a competitor. Why would they, when your path to a pleasurable experience is so clear and strong already? In this way, consistency allows customers to always know what they'll get from you. Your job is to ensure that every interaction with your brand is a positive one; one that evokes the emotions and feelings you want your audience to feel. Just be sure it's the same emotion every time. Remember, people crave consistency. If you can deliver that, they will constantly know what to expect from your brand and will reward you with sales.

Be Forceful About It

This entire book has been about driving consistency. It's about making sure your email signature, your brand colors, your office décor, your customer experience and your management style are all aligned. It's about making sure you use those elements to send the same exact message to everyone who interacts with your brand, both internally and externally. This is where a lot of companies come up short. Don't be one of them. Be a brand that knows what it stands for and consistently deliver that in everything and anything you do.

A good way to ensure that you're always being consistent is to appoint a dedicated brand enforcer. This person can either be an employee or an outside consultant, whose job is to review every element on your behalf, making sure each one remains on-brand. That individual must be ruthless about calling out inconsistencies. Yes, some people will be upset about having to redo work your brand enforcer has deemed to be "off-brand," but the adjustments will be worth it for the longevity of your brand. This person will need to comb through all of your materials, making sure they consistently elicit the kinds of reactions you're after, highlight the most important aspects of your brand and work seamless together. This is especially important during the initial twelve months of a brand launch and during a rebranding effort, since what you'll be doing is newly establishing yourself in the marketplace.

Engineer plays the brand enforcer role for the companies we work with. We do this to ensure the brand strategy that has been created for our clients actually comes to life as intended. We understand that business owners and the team of people directly working for the company have a lot on their plate. So when a new brand is being formed, it's helpful to have us there to keep the brand front and centre.

There is room for error, misinterpretation and, of course, falling back into old patterns when companies go about bringing their new brand to life. To combat that—and stay on-brand more easily—having a set of brand guidelines in place is crucial to help stay the course. Brand guidelines are basically your brand's bible. In print, electronic or a combination of formats, they lay out how your brand should always appear and be represented in visual and written form. This includes: How your logo is treated, what colors are used, how images are shot, which fonts are used where, which keywords matter, which words are to be avoided, etc. Your guidelines must also emphasize how consumers are meant to feel while and after they interact with your brand.

Anyone who works on your brand should be able to review your guidelines and instantly understand how (and how not) to treat it. Make reviewing them mandatory for any employee or contractor who'll have a hand in marketing and/or branding your business. The same goes for management teams and retail store supervisors. Print out a hard copy, load the pages in a binder and attach a signature page. Have them sign off, in agreement, after reviewing your guidelines.

Sections or elements typically included in a brand guideline book are:

- Your brand purpose or MTP
- Your logo and how it should be used

- Your brand colors, in exact pantone codes
- Your image choices: photos, illustrations, etc.
- Your brand tagline, including how/where it's used
- Your chosen keywords—plus brand words to avoid
- Your brand's associated emotions and characteristics
- Your font choices and settings (i.e., titles, text body, spacing)

Your guidelines binder should ultimately be designed to educate and guide anyone who will ever touch your brand, so they know how to treat it and are able to help you maintain its integrity. You must ensure that they have access to the book, reference it often and check their work against it before anything they do on your behalf goes out into the marketplace.

This may be the most important chapter of this entire book. If you walk away with only one thing after reading it in its entirety, walk away knowing that your brand must be stitched together across everything you do. Brand consistency is too often overlooked. Business owners assume—because they've nailed their logos or their partnerships or their office locations—that they're set to have long-lasting brands. What they forget are the little details, like how something gets delivered to a customer's door, what the checkout process is like or what appears in their email signatures. Details big and small are what separate good brands from great brands.

People love, respect and honor great brands. Be a great brand, by being consistent.

Brand-Building Touchpoints:

- Be consistent across everything you do.
- Be consistent about everything: big and small.
- Be consistent in how you present your brand to the world.

Your Brand Is Your Logo

What does your *logo* say about your brand?

I've intentionally made your logo the last element of your brand we discuss since, as you realize by now, your brand is *not* just your logo. I work with so many business owners who think they have their branding figured out. Why? Because they have a logo. Meanwhile, that image is rarely representative of what they want their brand to actually "be" for people. In addition, all the many other aspects of their brand have been left to the wayside.

Your logo is a part of your brand, yes, but it's by no means your brand in and of itself. Anyone who tries to sell you on a "branding package" by simply offering to design a logo for you and/or by presenting you with a few color options isn't actually aware of what branding is. Look for someone else who can help you build your brand, if you want it done right. This chapter briefly outlines what they and the right logo should help you achieve.

At a Glance

Your logo will tell people—with a quick glance—what your business is all about, what it stands for and what it can do for them. It's a stamp that announces who you are to the world. It should be a visual representation of what you offer, what your brand values and which emotions customers can look forward to experiencing. In order to create a successful logo, it's absolutely necessary to have a firm understanding of who you are, what you stand for and who you're speaking to. Your logo should be able to exist on its own and still hold meaning. When people look at it, it should evoke specific emotions in them. It should also communicate something about who you are.

Now, there are many ways to engineer your logo so that it lives and breathes alongside your business. The right choice for you will depend on (by now, you've guessed it): your brand. Some logos showcase a brand name. Others don't even include one. What works for someone else won't necessarily work for you and vice versa. Before you put any one logo into use, I encourage you to test out a few different options to see what truly *does* work for you, as well as your target audience. Things you want to consider include how your logo will look across all of your assets.

By that I mean everything your logo will touch: your website, your business cards, your letterhead, your marketing flyers, your print advertisements, your social media profiles and everything in between. Absolutely all of it. This particular consideration is important to keep in mind, as you begin building that logo. How will it look on packaging or shopping bags? Or on promotional items you choose to give away, as you begin spreading the word about your brand? It can be extremely dangerous to create a logo and then assess its strength in isolation. You need to know how it will actually live on your packaging and how it will look on other important brand materials like your website or marketing communication pieces.

The areas of this book which cover colors and typefaces will be key to reference, when you have your logo designed. The colors you choose should evoke the emotions you're going for. The font(s) you choose should also drive those same emotions, helping bring your brand to life even further. Sometimes it takes seeing what doesn't work to understand what does work. So, when building out your logo, try a wide variety of: colors, shades, tints, fonts, type styles and layouts.

Next Steps

There are other steps you need to take before launching your logo. For one, test that it's ownable by you and that you can legally lay claim to it. Look at competitors' logos and logos used by others who are in similar industries. Make sure that your own logo stands out and is distinct from the others. Like everything related to your brand, make it a point to avoid having your logo too closely resemble that of a competitor—or of anyone else, for that matter. You can use what others are doing as a guide, or as inspiration, but the reference shouldn't be an obvious one. Instead, look for ways you to make yours connect deeply and uniquely with your target market.

Don't worry if, after a few iterations, your logo still looks similar to others used in your industry. There's something to be said for that, too. If you look around, you'll probably notice that a lot of tech company logos feature a similar range of blues. That's because blue evokes the sorts of ideas, traits and characteristics associated with this category: trust, masculinity, advancement, security. If you run a tech company, those all serve as great motivation for wanting to use a similar blue in your own logo. There's nothing wrong with that line of thinking, but consider ways to distinguish yourself. Try a different shade of blue. Research other colors that communicate security and/or trust. Incorporate design elements and shapes that will do the same.

It's also helpful to think about what might visually represent what it is you offer. For example, Telegram is a cloud-based messaging service, which uses a paper airplane image set within a turquoise blue circle to showcase the idea that it's a fun, safe and secure form of communication. This out-of-the-box way of looking at what it offers makes the company stand out. By contrast, knowing there are lots of communication tools out there represented in blue, the Skype® logo more prominently features the letter "S." This automatically connects back to its brand name and, hopefully, the positive thoughts people associate with it.

Your Brand Logo

How do you know when you've arrived at the right logo? When you know what your brand is about and what it stands for, this becomes easier. Do the colors being used evoke the right emotions? Are they connected to your industry but not the exact same as everyone else's? Does the font choice represent your brand and bring about consumer reactions that make sense for your brand? Are the images used in your logo or logo layout clearly connected to your brand, what it represents and who you're speaking to? Does all of it make sense, given your target audience?

Let's try a little exercise to get you even closer to figuring this out. Write out all of the things your brand is. Now add all of the things you want your brand to stand for. Finally, list all of the emotions you want your brand to evoke in people. This is a good starting point, as you begin to consider what your logo could be. Once you have this list together, you can begin to imagine what may work well as a visual representation of you brand. The key here is to follow a process similar to the one we used when talking about your brand name. List out as many things as you can think of. Get creative. Get really creative! Go way out-of-the-box here.

This upfront list really has no wrong item on it. This is a true brainstorm at its finest. You will have a pile of ideas. Likely only a few can work. A few may even be *really* good. Yet, at times, it takes a pile of bad ideas to get to the really good ones. So, don't hold back. Once you're done, hand this over to the graphic designer or branding agency tasked with building your logo. After all, you wouldn't build a computer unless you were trained to. Likewise, don't attempt to build your logo yourself. You won't be doing the brand justice and everything you've created thus far can potentially be lost, unless you have training and experience related to graphic design.

Your logo is an important piece of the branding puzzle which, ideally, should represent your brand well on its own. However, to get to the point where your logo truly connects with your brand and consumers, you have to understand: who you are, what you stand for and who you're speaking to. Why are you in business? What tangible and intangible benefits does your product or service offer? Why? Who are your best customers, how can you truly connect with them and where will you do that?

While your brand is *not* just your logo, be sure to use all of your answers to the questions above and all of the work you've done in earlier chapters to inform your logo design. Because, when it comes to building an indelible brand, it's a key element that gives visual representation to who you are across everything you do. When you consider the role it plays, as a point of reference anywhere people encounter may it, it's too important to overlook.

Brand-Building Touchpoints:

- Understand your brand well before building your logo.
- Use colors, fonts and images which evoke related emotions.
- Work with a skilled designer, saving yourself both time and worry.

CONCLUSION

All of it adds up to *your* brand.

Your brand is everything your business does. It's every email, every ad, every hire and, yes, it's embedded in your logo. The key to building a strong brand is to actually take the time to think about all of these elements and every little detail within them. This is something not everyone does. It's something most people don't even think about doing. Or, when they do think about it, they only consider those aspects of brand building that they can quickly identify.

They've got the logo, font and colors down. Yet, they struggle with the little details, which can elevate a brand and take it from good to great. The little details are the difficult ones to address. They aren't considered immediately impactful, so they're easily overlooked. In most cases, overlooking them results in mediocre brands that fail to consistently deliver on brand promises and leave consumers lacking a sense of loyalty to them.

Engineering your brand is not an overnight task. And it's not something that'll drive sales to you immediately. What it will do is allow you to stand out from competitors, build lasting relationships with consumers and develop a brand that lasts over time. You must be dedicated and completely committed to your brand, building it into everything you and your company does. You must live and breathe it—ensuring that everyone who's involved in creating your brand buys into it, as well.

A great way to keep your brand at the forefront, so that it informs all you do, is to surround yourself with meaningful reminders that keep you connected to your brand. Examples include:

- Your logo – *Print it, frame it and hang it high!*
- Your goals – *What got you started on this journey?*
- Your target audience – *Remind yourself who this is often.*
- Your Massive Transformative Purpose – *Read it often.*
- Your motivation – *Why must your brand exist for people?*
- Your results – *Keep a client Thank You note or gift nearby.*
- Your solution – *Remember what problem your brand solves.*

What gets us excited to keep moving our brands along is different for every person. It may even be different depending on your business type. The key is to find something that visually reminds you of the need for consistency and the need to bring your brand to life across everything you do. The in-store experience should not be more important than the follow-up to a purchase. Your initial sales meeting shouldn't outshine the experience of opening a product package. All are necessary to build brand love and to build your brand into a holistic, functioning symbol of your business aspirations.

If you want to build not just any brand—but a truly great brand—I hope you'll use this book as a guide for doing just that. By paying attention to all of the little things your competitors are ignoring, you'll secure a more prominent and lasting place in people's minds, hearts and wallets.

And that's the goal, seeing as great brands don't just happen. *They're engineered!*

About the Author

Ainsley Moir is the Founder and Chief Brand Engineer at Engineer Your Brand, a company dedicated to building and growing impactful brands and profitable businesses. With a focus on strategy and developing brands, Engineer Your Brand works as a partner to companies to ensure they don't just create a business, they create lasting brands that connect with people.

Taking learning and frameworks from Fortune 500 companies and adapting these for businesses of all sizes, Ainsley shares with the people she works how they can build a powerful brand and set their business up for success.

If you have branding questions this book didn't cover, feel free to send a direct email to Ainsley@EngineerYourBrand.com or visit the website www.EngineerYourBrand.com.

Manufactured by Amazon.ca
Bolton, ON

23274844R00111